DEDI

This book is dedicated to God; the staff and volunteers of Open Doors and The Leprosy Mission; and the millions of Christians worldwide, who are tortured, jailed, killed or exiled from their families but refuse to deny God or relinquish their faith.

TRIGGER WARNINGS

Suicide, abuse, domestic violence, bullying, miscarriage, school shootings and divorce.

You're holding a mixed bag of poetry; short silly poems of only a few words; sentimental poems; raw poems about surviving trauma and poems about faith.

These are messy. Several would be panned by critics or fail to get past the first round of any literary contest BUT they are honest, easy to understand and are a splatter painting of my life.

The book also charts my journey from passionately hating God/religion/the Bible to (without hearing a sermon or being influenced by a single Christian) deciding to live God's way; asking him to forgive my sins and wanting to live with him at the centre of my life.

The collection covers time before and after becoming a Christian, including days where I've failed miserably. It describes days where my mental health is still a challenge and days when I think of random thoughts such as 'What would I ask Ben Nevis?'

This might be the last bunch of poetry I ever publish or write…but since the age of fourteen I've tried 'giving up poetry' unsuccessfully…it still has a stubborn, relentless habit of catching up with you eventually.

I pray and hope you enjoy this. I hope you realise that others struggle too. Most importantly I hope you see that you matter to God.

Second most importantly I hope you realise that if an eejit like me can publish a book, anyone can.

HANDSHAKE

Hey you,

With the weird imagination and odd ways!

You with your kitchen-dancing, singing, creative, book-obsessed, feeling-like-Peter -Pan, approach to life.

You with the parts of yourself that others

Have labelled eccentric or 'different'…

You're a bloomin' marvellous, strange, interesting, bundle of possibilities and I think you're wonderful.

If we're not already,

Let's be friends.

RIGHT NOW

Right now there are good, great, merciful,
Loving and compassionate actions happening.

Right now, people are proposing, others are making a stand;
while others still are hearing 'I love you' for the first time.
Children are being born, people are saying 'I do' and several
million people are giggling.

A few thousand are experiencing God's love and peace for
the first time.

Right now people are also hurting or being hurt, wounding,
killing, dying, grieving; breaking up or realising something is
over.

Millions of people are crying.

Right. Now.

So right now, I remember that God is love, calling me to
serve and love others. Right now, I want to make the world a
better place, even in some small way; in my family, street
and community.

Right. Now.

FIZZY TO FLAT LINE

I spent the first five weeks of being a Christian,
floating on air.
Electricity charged from my toes to my
Crown; buzzing with a peace, joy and
Power I hadn't known before.
Prayers, conversations and time with God
Came so easily.
Answered prayers dropping like
Rescue packages, parachuted in daily.
I read Christian books, sang Worship songs
And the giddy, re-found love of God
Meant I couldn't stop thinking about him.
I started having hopes for the future;
Seeing a galaxy of possibility every day
And feeling a yearning to preach and teach.
Then Shhhhhhhh.
It was all so quiet.
I still read my Bible; I needed to.
I still prayed daily. I read my daily devotions
And still occasionally sang worship songs
BUT all the Holy-shiver, vibrations and
Electricity had stopped.
The feel-good motivation and sunny
Disposition was nowhere to be found.

I felt guilty. I felt condemned. I doubted.
I couldn't find any answers so I decided to
Keep going, even when I didn't feel like it.
I decided to pray as a discipline
Rather than as a feeling.
I decided that just maybe, this was the
Beginning of me growing up so I needed
To trust and know God was there, regardless.
I'm still in the flat-line, unmotivated stage
But I know God is faithful, God is present,
And he wants me to trust my knowledge
Of him.
(Written September 2022.)

TRUST.

That word again *trust!*

I knew I trusted God.

I believed Jesus died on the cross then

Came back to life.

I knew the Bible was God's word.

I trusted God with my future didn't I?!

The more I thought about it,

I found myself telling God that I wasn't sure

If I trusted anyone one-hundred percent.

That I'd had so many people hurt me or let me down, when I trusted them.

That I always allowed that final ten or five

Percent to be held back because

Maybe there'd be less chance of being hurt.

I sat in silence for a while, crying…

I found myself saying

'I'm scared to trust you'

And heard God say that he already knew.

He wasn't going anywhere.

The promises in the Bible are true and that

He just needed me to be honest.

I said 'I think I can.'

HIS HANDS

His hands are in mine.
My heart is on the line.
In his grasp I feel divine;
I'm his, he's mine...
And if the world should fall apart
I know he'll still have my heart;
And when no one understands
I have his hands.

THE DAY AFTER I KILLED MYSELF

The day after I killed myself, I woke and skipped breakfast, as I usually do,until I walked past Tesco and bought two Chelsea buns, on the way to meet friends.

We laughed, gossiped and for once I told them I was really struggling. They listened and promised to check in later that week.

I bought some canvasses and a new notebook so I could start writing and painting again. Before I knew it, it was fiveish so I made tea and went for a walk.

I watched the sunset and noticed five different shades of red , before going to the morgue so I could plead with myself to wake up.

To shout and bargain with myself to wake up to the good things waiting.

But the body; cold, grey and still, refused to listen to my cries for help.

It couldn't hear me.

DOES T.V EVER GET AS GOOD AS WHEN YOU'RE A KID?

I feel like I'm part of the final generation

To whom T.V was golden;

No pausing.

No catch up services.

Just using blank VHS tapes

to record films or telly occasionally.

Between the late seventies

And late eighties

We had reruns of all the best stuff;

Usually from America…

Knightrider, Fall Guy, MacGyver,

The A Team, Airwolf, Streethawk, Spider Man, The Incredible Hulk, Fame, DeGrassi Junior High, Happy Days, CHiPS, Starsky and Hutch…

Programmes full of action,

With no blood or death;

Just merchandise 'tie ins';

A hundred toys you'd pray

You'd receive,

for Christmas.

And the cartoons!!!…

He-Man, She-Ra, Dogtanian, Mr Ben,

G-Force, M.A.S.K, Transformers, GoBots, Prince Valiant,
Bravestar, The Family Ness, Morph, Danger Mouse,
Superted, Bananaman, The Muppet Babies...

These were the 'Saturday morning,

Tiptoe downstairs' shows,

'to let mum and dad have a lie in,

Slurping Weetabix and managing my siblings shows'.

Then there were the afternoon shows...

Byker Grove, Grange Hill, Blue Peter,

Morph, Pigeon Street, Record Breakers, Mr Benn...

As I got slightly older there were...

...Teenage Mutant Ninja (Hero) Turtles, The Simpsons,
Fresh Prince and then there

Was Quantum Leap, which sparked us to want to live in
others' skins,

Travelling back in time...

I loved them all.

They filled my dreams and sparked

Drawings and bike rides and hours

Played with cars in my room.

They represent Christmases and

Hoped-for wishes...

Maybe it was the once a week rarity.

Maybe it was because for all the rubbish

That comes with childhood -

Bullying, being in trouble, being poor,

Mum and Dad's arguments; or the crippling

Anxiety (that had me suffering insomnia)

That it was a solace, a brain break,

A hushhhhh of being purely in the present.

No 'on demand or streaming services or Tik Tok or YouTube 'celebrities',

will ever compare…

And I feel sorry for my kids

That they didn't get to live

When kids' T.V was king.

BECAUSE I HAVE READ

I have travelled in time;

Explored the past

And seen the future in

Chrome and neon-lights

I have slayed beasts, been hunted and

Seen the world through a thousand pensive eyes.

I have faced my biggest fears, ran away;

And loved and lost and been unloved.

I have been immortal.

I have lived briefly and re-animated in different times and places.

I have travelled, remained and

Been lost with no way out.

I have lived

Because I have read.

PARENTS EVENING

I taught in a special needs school years ago.
One of the parents of a boy who's behaviour
And moderate learning difficulties,
Made a few snide remarks about her son,
Who regularly attended school in
Unwashed clothes...
I deflected and changed the subject
As she openly badmouthed him,
While he sat (on the verge of tears) next to her.

She was my last appointment
And as I left the building,
She was waiting for a taxi...
...I heard her shouting at my student...
The only words I caught were:
'Stupid', 'idiot', 'horrible' and 'fat.'
As a dad, it made me so angry.

It changed how I taught him after that.
It taught me to use these evenings
To learn what my students needed
Beyond their school-learning;
To watch their parents more closely.
To remember that words have power;

That I could change the words forming

Their identity:

'valued', 'clever', 'kind', 'helpful', 'resilient' and 'important'.

A PLANK IN CHURCH

I noticed the clothes people were wearing
but missed the prayers.
I noticed the crying children and parenting
But missed the meaning of the songs.
I noticed the breathing and whispering
But missed the testimony shared.
I noticed the yellow teeth and latecomers
But missed the sermon.
I noticed the people, the temperature, the
Attitudes, the voices, the scowls, the
Joyless attitudes, the boredom, the old
Fashioned songs.....then left,
Moaning about not sensing God's presence.

As I walked out, the two-by-four
In my eye kept hitting the pillars and the
Door frames.

NAMING THE TREES ON OUR STREET

I tolerate the audio-sensitivity
And mild hand tremors.
I just about cope with nudges by
Feral toddlers chasing each other.
I manage to wince at the sun in my eyes
For the joy of seeing her face.

See, I'm aware that this ten minutes
Of cacophony and crowds
mightn't seem much
But my undiagnosed, latent autism
Means this overwhelms my senses.
When she comes out, I wave
And she points with a 'my dad's there'
Before I laugh at the ridiculousness
Of her wearing a coat over her backpack.

Me and tiny Quasimodo amble home,
Arms swinging, while we chat;
What she had for lunch, who she played with, which lessons
she enjoyed and what she learnt.
I am fully present. I hope she remembers these days and
treasures them like I will.
The playground panic attack seems a distant memory,

While we near home,
trying to think of the names of the
trees on our street.

A PRAYER FOR MY FRIENDS AND FAMILY...

May you find peace in the turmoil,

May you find hope when all feels lost.

May you see the possibilities,

May you see the invisible 'what will be' when people or situations seek to destroy you.

May this poem remind you that pain and darkness is often a precursor to growth.

May you find strength when exhausted,

May you find love when feeling unloveable

May you see the good and great you do in the world, even when you feel like a failure.

May you know I'm always here for you;

whether you need to chat, rant or laugh.

May you find sanity in the madness.

May you find friendship when isolated.

May you see that you've barely tapped the incredible potential within you.

May you know God's love, acceptance,

healing, forgiveness and peace.

WEIGHTLESS

I notice myself praying sometimes
'Dear God, please help me with...';
Then I list all my hurt, mistakes, labels,
Weaknesses, trauma and guilt.
I've realised that for so long
I've been wrong in those prayers.
See, God doesn't want to just
Lend a hand.
God doesn't just want to
Reach around to your backpack
Of rubbish and weight,
Only to just lift it slightly.
He doesn't want to just help
Or take one or two items.
He simply wants us to
Hand the rucksack over to him.
The bullying, the abuse,
the names repeated to yourself,
the heartbreak,
The lies, the betrayal, the emotional
And physical scars.
He wants it all.
Whether we're already Christians or not
He calls to us:

'Come to me all who are weary and I will give you rest.'
We don't have to keep shouldering
This energy-sapping, back-breaking
Load any more.
He wants us to offer it to him...
...and he'll take care of the rest.

IN HARMONY

I watch him take her hand, kissing her veined wrist, then lean into her ear

Whispering to a barely perceptible hearing aid. She laughs, coyly and looks down, like the night they met in nineteen forty-two.

She mouths something and he stands, while helping her; supporting her elbow.

The song has begun and as they step near a busy, twirling, congested, newly polished dance floor they automatically hold each other as they did that first night; he moves forward, her feet move back. He gently leans one way and she follows.

As I keep watching I see her gaze up at him with a look that comes with decades of hard work, knowing and forgiving. I notice her directing him with her eyes and subtle hand gestures. Embarrassed, I turn to leave as she bursts out laughing, as he suggests dancing to another song.

WINTER HAIKU

Freezing cold evenings
Under mountains of blankets;
Fire purring softly

GOD IS THE CURE

To loneliness
To truth blindness
To the uninspired
To the lost
To dis-connection
To ambivalence
To the searching
To apathy
To the silence
To the noise
To the hopeless
To being fake
To forgetting
To giving up
To sin
To thinking it's all so...
Pointless

SHE STILL THINKS I COULD LEAVE HER

She tells me that she worries I'll leave her.
That I might find a better option.
That the greener grass might be taken.
That in some alternate reality I demand
A refund.

She still doesn't realise that to leave her
Would tear my soul in two.

That like a symbiotic creature; I have become her and she has become me.

Melded.

She doesn't realise that she is my magnetic north, drawing me to the home that is her.

WE CAN STAND IN SILENCE...

Can I stand beside you for a while my friend?

Can I hold your bag, to give your shoulders a rest?

Can I hold an umbrella over you so the heat is less intense?

We can stand in silence; we don't need to talk.

Can I listen to your problems and what's spinning in your head?

Can I talk about old times or stuff we still find funny?

Can I get you something to sit on so you can rest and breathe.

We can stand in silence; we don't need to talk.

Can I hold your hand for a while my friend?

Can you tell me about the thoughts that spin in your head at one a.m?

Can you shout or cry or rant without feeling I'll judge you? (I won't)

We can stand in silence; we don't need to talk.

Can you hold on for one more day my friend?

Can you promise to please try and find help?

Can you be honest with yourself and get the support you need?

We can stand in silence; we don't need to talk.

A POET WITH WRITER'S BLOCK

My brain has wilted,
My creativity has melted.
My mind has turned to jelly.
My concentration, diluted.
My spark has been snuffed.
My sharpness is blunted.
My pops and explosions have fizzled out.
My inspiration has become perspiration.
My words have been silenced.
My eyes are unaware.
My ears are full of wax.
My optimism has turned to pessimism.
My fizzy drink is flat.
My rhymes are past their 'use by' date.
My focus has become cloudy.
My wonder, has wandered.
So I wrote a poem about it.

FIERY (FOR GRANDAD JOHN)

His face turned a purple, maroon red
'I can handle ma heat' he said.
Sitting there chewing and licking through
Wings and sauces and marinated meat;
Eyes streaming,
I asked my step-dad
'Are you ok?
How's the heat?'
With tingling, burning lips
And a constricted voice,
He croaked;
'Fiery'

THE GIFT OF CHOICE

At the end of my first year of university,

I went to see the head of our faculty-

A squat, smiley, steel-willed, Welsh woman

Called Jean.

I'd had counselling but my brain was still throwing itself against the walls of my skull,

Desperate to escape, shut down; to get away.

I had paranoia filled pockets; a backpack of self-doubt and hands that shook like an alcoholic, twenty-four hours into his first

Sober day.

My life and thoughts were spiralling, running away from me; chasing me like the boulder in temple of doom, while everybody else seemed carefree.

I nervously thanked her for seeing me and told her how sorry I was but that I needed to

Quit the course, explaining the reasons;

She listened.

At the end of it she looked at my crumpled form and told me gently that it would be very easy to arrange and that I was free

To choose.

This wisest of women understood that I needed to grasp choice (or control) and to feel like it was me who was deciding my future; not my anxiety.

She started shuffling papers and informed me that I should come back in one or two days to officially hand in my forms; I never did.

THE BATTLE OF THE SPROUTS (AND HOW TO EAT SPROUTS DURING CHRISTMAS DINNER)

I. Hate. Sprouts.

Not a 'slightly dislike' or 'I'm not keen' but a full blown, rage-fuelled hatred.

As a child it was a case of 'tough, it's been bought and made for you' by a Yorkshire mum, teaching us the values of not wasting food.

I sat there, year on year, retching and gipping with my parents merely advising 'have a drink after a sprout' so it was:

Schloer- Sprout

Sprout-Schloer

X 4

I tried making sprout scotch-eggs with mash encasing them. Just made the beautiful, creamy mash, rancid.

I tried covering them in cranberry sauce (non-left for the turkey), shredding them (made them gross AND cold) or the final approach that I use now….

Eat them quick, after putting all 3 or 4 in your mouth, swallow, big swig of Schloer, enjoy my meal.

As a dad who makes my kids (who bloomin' love sprouts) eat all their food daily- they love watching me gip, retch and bauk on Christmas Day.

Ho. Ho. Ho.

DOOR ONE

On day zero of this advent period

I approach my Cadburys advent calendar with salivating anticipation at seven a.m

With gentle dexterity, I accept my fingers are like sausages so I'm extra careful.

I open the cardboard door to a quiet rip as the perforation pops.

On the inside of the door there's a picture of a muffin.

I then press out the chocolate shaped like a ginger bread man and instead of decapitating him, remove his limbs;

I then let him sit on my tongue,

Melting away…..

I grab my coffee and cornflakes and sit by the window watching snow fall, as though I'm in a giant snow globe.

This month is a clean, fresh slate.

DARK MORNING

I woke today
And wore you like
My favourite coat
Refusing to turn the lights on
(So I could see the frost twinkle
Its diamond dust on leaves)
I spied the world
Safe from the kitchen window
watching the sun rise
as the moon stubbornly stayed,
Refusing to leave the night.

LET'S PLAY (MADE IN GOD'S IMAGE)

Let's live creatively today!
Let's marvel and wonder.
Let's ask hundreds of questions,
Even if it's just using our
'Inside voices'.
Let's commit to creating
Those things that
Lift our souls and minds,
(With no tense, nervous
Holding on to desired
Outcomes.)
Let's bravely, ferociously,
Playfully,
make, explore or
Experiment...
Let's not think beyond
The present-moment joy.
Let's not second guess
Or *over*think.
Let's look for the odd or small
Details we usually miss.
Let's make up songs walking to the shops.
Let's write down (or draw) something
that we think is beautiful.

Let's dance in our kitchen as though
a whole theatre were watching us,
while we smash it.
Let's start to make notes
(on paper or in our phones)
about that thing we really want to create;
the idea that just won't go away.
Let's work solo or collaboratively.
Let's be fearless in knowing most of what we'll create is
purely for practice
or our 'in the moment' enjoyment.
Let's do for the sake of doing
But most importantly, creatively;
Let's play.

FORGIVENESS

I struggle with forgiveness.
The unfairness of giving someone
A gift they neither deserve
Or, sometimes, even want.
I wrestle with people who don't even
See their faults or mistakes...
Putting yourself out there,
Forgiving, accepting and choosing
To love them regardless.
It's hard.
It's near impossible.
It's painful...
But I know I've been forgiven
And I'm so undeserving of forgiveness.
I know I regularly make mistakes,
Which lets God down...
So with his strength I'll forgive
Then forgive some more.
I've received so much that
I must love, as he first loved me.

THINK ON ALL THAT IS GOOD, NOBLE AND PRAISEWORTHY (PHILIPPIANS 4:8)

My wife's compassionate heart.

My daughters' smiles,

The sea at dusk or dawn.

The cooling air after a storm.

Kindness, courage and hope.

God's Grace.

Forgiveness.

The wild scenery of north-western Scotland.

Beaches in Wales;

rugged and full of sand dunes.

Mercy, second chances and love.

My sons' tenacity and affection.

Watching dolphins in the sea.

Being content and satisfied.

Hugs from my family.

Swimming. Running. Dancing.

Good food, shared with friends.

Peace, that passes understanding.

POETRY IS...

Blood letting
Mind selfies
Pen weeping
Hope giving
Raw honesty
Magic weaving
Ripples expanding
Seeds planting
Words dancing
Political ranting
Artistic chanting
Minds connecting
Society reflecting
Feathers ruffling
Diamond mining
Brain rain
Mind moulting
Self therapy
Floatation device
Spirit soaring
Free styling
Rhythm beating
Powerful penmanship
Many faces

Lyrical exploration
Scorching truths
Soothing lies
Eyes opened
Loneliness easing
Brain teasing
Heart unfreezing
Lexicon addiction
Written friction
Pure joy!

PERSPECTIVE

She tells me I'm distant and
Haven't been affectionate.
I remember specific times
Where I have been...
But I struggle to remember things.
In her reality, I've been stand-offish,
Cold and different...
In my mind, I've been really tired
And just a bit low but overall,
I've had a good week. I think.
Are we both wrong?
Are we both seeing the same
thing from different angles
Or is it simply her turn
To be paranoid?

THE GLASS IS HALF EMPTY...

My mum told me
She was proud of
Me today and that
She loved me...
all I could think to say about
It to my wife was...
'I hope that doesn't mean
She's dying'.

FEATHER

I stroked yer hair while singing auld, Scottish folk songs,
While your ma showered;
I silently wept in the relief that only comes
Fae seeing a nurse untie the umbilical cord
From around your neck, as you were born.
The relief that comes from surviving all your ma's bleeds.
The relief that comes fae nine months ae
Pleading to a god I didn't yet believe in.
While rocking you, looking at your face,
I repeated your name like a prayer
Daring to believe in heaven.
Your mum came out the shower and I found
A single white feather;
It must have been from where your wings
Once were.

MAUSOLEUM

The garden's become a museum or graveyard of memories…

What looks like a collection of old, broken junk is actually a memoriam of magical moment-holders.

The chipped, plastic blue table that all four kids sat at, while toddlers.

The spinner toy that went in to next door's garden and on the garage roof.

The outdoor brush that I set on fire during one of our fire pits.

The rusty shovel the boys used when sorting the garden one summer to earn spending money to go on a day trip to the sea, on their own.

The goals that were played with for hours and opened excitedly on Christmas morning.

The pile of cardboard boxes that were presents or spent birthday vouchers or dens.

The pile of drift-wood, foraged from the seashore on family walks.

The punch bag and gloves from various keep fit stages and teaching the kids to defend themselves.

The four slice toaster in chrome that made hundreds of morning breakfasts until it electrocuted my wife.

The laughter, games, meals and joy and work that these items hold sitting in the garden, decaying.

It causes me to worry that, one day, when the kids have left home, our house will feel the same.

WINTER'S EVE

She asks me again
'Is it winter tomorrow Dad?'
I tell her it is and her face
Lights up, reminding me that
In the morning she will
Greet me with
'Happy Winter Dad!'
She teaches me to hope,
Celebrate change and value
The seasons,
On this rainy
'Winter's Eve'

A POEM THAT SHINES

You
Are
Loved
And
You
Have
Something
Unique
To
Offer
The
World;
You
Beautiful,
Talented,
Wonderful,
Person.

THE DECADENT DREAMS OF A PARENT

Some people dream of Ferraris; multi-million dollar yachts; trips to space or having a mansion on every continent.

Some people dream of Cristal champagne, caviar and oysters, while sat in a luxury 300th floor restaurant; followed by extortionate cocktails, mixing with celebrities….

…But me?

I just want a poo in peace.

HEAVY LOAD.

Movie stars achieve fame, millions of dollars, mansions, adoration and anything they desire…only to take overdoses to kill the feelings of emptiness.

Marriages end in divorce at an increasing rate - consumer, swipe-left culture reigns.

Drugs become easier to acquire; to silence the dark thoughts or gorge on experiences, that never last.

Governments talk about saving the planet, while doing nothing about the greed or poverty that interrupts those efforts.

People look within for a bunch of answers, only to feel depressed when all their reading, soul-searching and self-analysis produces nothing that lasts.

In every village, town and city throughout the world, people are addicted, people are lonely and people hunger to own things in the vain hope that these temporary possessions satisfy them.

Still other people wear blinkers that convince themselves that it's only what is physically in front of them that exists; never explaining the emptiness or lack of satisfaction they refuse to admit.

People build their happiness on things *that were never designed to bear the weight*; relationships, having kids, careers and achievements…only to find that when these fail or fall…there's an empty echo…

ALL of these are symptoms of a world that needs God.

ALL of these will persist until we realise our compass's true North was always God - to be in a right relationship with him.

We can run, gorge on pleasure, ignore, argue it away but NONE of these things will ever, truly satisfy or bring peace; only God can do that.

Only God can forgive you.

Only God can fill that 'God shaped hole' in your heart.

WOMB

You knew me
And created me
Before I even inhaled
My first breath.
You knitted me together
And have a purpose for me.
I am not a mistake.
I am fearfully and wonderfully
Made.
(Psalm 139:14)

IMPORTANT ORDERS

A soldier's orders are non-negotiable, clear, plainly given and not-to-be-argued with.

Centuries ago, such things would also be done when a King or Queen gave their subjects an instruction.

It makes me wonder why so many people (including myself) then struggle to follow Jesus TWO main instructions:

'Love the Lord, your God, with all your heart, soul and mind;

AND

'Love your neighbour as yourself.'

We can only do this in God's strength but any refusal to do this is disobedience;

It is refusal to follow our King, who gave *his* very life, to take the punishment for *our* sins…how could we dare disobey?

FAITH IS AN EXERCISE IN TRUST.

It's a baby bird, jumping out a nest that learns to fly by being willing to leap.

It's cordial/squash/diluting juice that, when added to living water, grows and flows.

It's Indiana Jones stepping out in 'The last crusade', trusting the invisible bridge;

Trusting the words in an old book.

It's looking up not down.

It's a winter's fire, being breathed to life by Holy Bellows…sparking embers to a roar.

It's baby's steps that become firmer through trust in a parent; falling then getting up again and again.

It's having open eyes to see the world as it truly is and can be.

LET'S PRETEND (THIS ISN'T HAPPENING IN OUR SOCIETY)

A student takes food out their plastic bag and eats their handful of items ravenously with chomps and slurps…only close inspection reveals the occasional tap and 'clack', as they pretend to eat the plastic food their mom sent them in with.

There was no money for lunch this week.

Another students performs practiced mime skills as they take take empty packets of crisps, cellophane, biscuit wrappers and empty miniature raisin boxes; rushing to force empty, invisible food into empty, visibly shrinking, bellies.

There was no money for lunch this week.

One five year-old girl opens a lunch box containing bread, dotted and smudged with blue and green mould. She furtively looks around, hoping no one notices her retch or meticulously picking the mould off.

There was no money for fresh food this week.

In another school a child refills their beaker of water four or five times; 'the two slim pieces of cheese will last longer that way'; at least that's what their mum told them.

There was no money for lunch this week.

I need to tell you *'these kids aren't from parents who are addicts, on benefits or jobless'*….these children are from families where the parent (or parents) have jobs.

Teachers, who are struggling themselves, are buying food to help students they care about.

These kids are struggling to concentrate to even achieve or meet basic attainment in subjects, due to lack of energy…

…and despite knowing this, our government does…

…*nothing!*

(Written November 2022)

PSALM 2022

Abba father; dear God

Things are hard right now.

People are using food banks to survive; energy companies are making money by crushing the poor under increasing costs; our government doesn't seem to care.

Lord, I struggle some days, feeling anxious about the cost of living crisis, global warming, strikes and a lack of empathy from those tasked with leading.

You oh God, are worthy. You have set my feet on a rock, promising that you are with me. I will not be afraid and I trust your word.

Calum x

MY EYES ARE FIXED ON HIM

I've been outrageous and courageous;
I've failed and bombed the test.
Though in knots and ink blots;
I've been blessed, though pressed…
Compacted.
Enacted panicked cries to God.
Shepherding and protecting me
With his staff and rod.
Though I'm nervous I'm singing;
My heart drenched in peace.
Since the day I cried out,
I've felt release
and though I'm
Far from perfect,
He's the Lord of me;
My strength, shield and stronghold,
My soul feels free.
At times low or dejected
I'm never rejected.
This relationship is something
I never wanted or expected.
Thunder roars; storms come
In a howling gale
But my God is in the boat;

Yes I will regale
The stories of hope.
How he made me free.
My father, my God;
Who calms the sea.

MAY PRAYER 3

Dear God,

I feel like a real failure today. I've been swearing again. I've been proper freaking out about my health stuff and having the shakes. Despite all the stuff I've learnt since being a Christian, one health scare has me panicking!

The failure's weighing me down with a tonne-load of guilt and shame.

My prayer life has been awful. I've been judgemental again and I've been struggling in not resisting the urge to moan to Laura about people I feel let down by.

How did you do it? Like, years and years of close friends letting you down - it seems so impossible and exhausting.

I'm sorry for the ways I've let you down recently. I'm sorry for the times I've tried to rely on my own strength, rather than yours. I'm just so tired of the guilt and messing up.

My mind keeps goading me saying I should 'pack it all in' and that I'll 'always be a failure'; I know that's not true though. I know I'll never be good enough and never was. I can only boast in what you've done for me.

Thank you for never giving up on me.

Calum

STRAIGHT JACKET

Who decided straight jackets
Should be white?
Who made the rule that robbers'
Masks must be black?
Where is my consultant in a
Technicolour dream (lab) coat?
Where is the local vicar in a beautiful
Red (or black) velvet collar?
Who decided hospital scrubs
Should be blue?
Who made the rule that certain
Districts' lights would be red?
Where is the nun wearing a
Sequinned, pink habit?
Where is the iconography
Of Jesus with sandy or brown skin?
Where are the goths wearing
Yellow, green and beige?

WHAT WILL YOU DO?!!

What will you do,
When you run out of road;
When you're at the rope's end
And it has no hope to give?
What will you do,
When your life's imploded;
When the cries for answers
Seem to die in the air?
What will you do,
When your goals are all met;
When the sweet satisfaction
Now meets with thin air?
What will you do,
When there are no answers;
When the world who promised much
Is now curled up, asleep?
What will you do,
Now the promises were cheap?

I WAS BORN IN…..

A darkened alley, as hissed air vents
Above me rained enveloping, warm
clouds.
There, among the Madness bounces;
Rod Stewart struts and Jagger shakes,
I *entered* this world;
Delivered by a cackling Jamaican woman *prophesying*:
'he's got a big mouth, like his father'
Among damp boxes, broken glass and darkness,
foreshadowing my years as a toddler.
I *arrived* shouting, screaming,
Demanding to be heard -
I am here.
I am here.
Hear me.

LOAD BEARING

Guilt
Is the silent killer
That will drill into your head.
Spin in your mind,
Constant rewind,
Swapping praise with thoughts of dread.

Guilt
is the slow, suffocater;
That will stop you being able to breathe.
It stops Holy air
From you being aware
That **you** can order these thoughts to leave.

Guilt
Is the stealthy assassin
That quietly slips into your heart.
It dares you to stop.
It taunts that you're worthless.
It says you're a failure so
Why bother to re-start.
Guilt
Is the chafing chain
That will squeeze you and keep you still.

It says this is pointless

And a waste of your time.

You're protected so it's your *faith*, the devil tries to kill.

JANUARY 2022 PRAYER

Dear God,

There's so much I still struggle with; impatience, pride, irritability and swearing. I hate disappointing you and wish I could just never sin or offend you.

Please forgive me and please help me because I can't do any of it without your power.

I want to be more like you but my old self tries to wrestle control back, determined to be self sufficient and to fight my own corner.

I struggle to be truly humble in putting others and you first.

Please help me.

Thanks for being patient.

Calum

READING MY NEW BIBLE

The edges crackle;
Electricity surging through its pages.
This is not some dead tome.
This is not some ancient, irrelevant text.
Thunder, wind and rain blast from your pages.
Light illuminates the parts of me
That need to be seen;
Shining truth and direction.
My fingers, stained with truth and love,
Make me smile, as my hands reverberate;
As God reminds, chides and instructs me.
God's true Word.
Alive, breathing, true and relevant;
Awe-inspiring and
Divine.

ODE TO A HEAVENLY FATHER

I look to your handiwork
That shouts its praise to you
Oh God.
The rolling power and
Serene peace of the sea.
The jagged, carved, strength
Of the mountains.
I look to the fine threads of
A spider's web or a leaf's veins.
The varied, rich, multiple shades
Of each colour; gloriously pointing
To a God who declared
'It is good'.

GOD. ANSWERS. PRAYER.

I have seen 'small' things answered
And huge situations changed.
I have seen answers to prayer
Where the chances of it happening
Are one in a billion.
People may say that
These things are easily-explained
'Coincidences'
But it's amazing how much these
'Coincidences' happen
When I pray.
God hears. God cares.
God. Answers. Prayer

SCI-FI PARABLE: WHAT WILL YOU BUILD ON?

On a planet, not so far away
The people scraped, grabbed and toiled
To build lives;
They looked to love, family, careers, pleasure, friendships,
fame, success, power, money and sex on which
To build purpose, identity and meaning.
The planet's inhabitants didn't realise
That all these things were too weak
To bear such weight.
Over time and during fierce storms,
These 'buildings' and 'attempts' simply
Fell apart.
One group however, seemed to build
On stronger foundations that despite
The storms and harsh conditions
Stood strong.
Their secret? They'd simply followed
The creator's instructions…
Despite the scoffing and mocking of others,
They built their lives on him.
…and the houses on the rock stood firm.

WHEN YOU FEEL THE SQUEEZE...

When an orange is squeezed, pressed and crushed, *what comes out?*

When an apple is pulped in one of those posh cafes; destroyed and spun; *what comes out?*

If you take a bunch of blueberries in your hand and mash, squish and squash them; *what comes out?*

Then why, when I feel crushed, pressed, spun and squeezed, do things come out of me that aren't like Christ; *anger, fear, temper, irritability and panic...*

Lord please make me more like you so when I'm under pressure, what comes out is completely, recognisably, like you.

BUZZIN'

You came home today,
Buzzin' about a beekeeper
That visited your year two class.

You rattled off facts, their preferred flowers
And how many bees are needed
To make a full, jar of honey.

You told me, smiling,
That you need to give sugary water
If bees look tired.

You told me about the beeswax candle
The lady brought in;
How amazing it was, that bees made it.

Then you and your sister showed
Me the first three strawberries of summer
And we ate them, feeling grateful;

Proudly agreeing,
Our strawberries are better than
Any you can buy from the local shop.

My beautiful, arty, bee-loving girl,
I desperately, hopefully, and optimistically
Pray that you keep this wonder
And amazement until you're old and grey.

PRESENT AND CORRECT

I shift my bum to get comfortable
In the collapsible, used-to-be-white chair;
The garden is quiet apart from a rushing wind.
Golden leaves flutter from trees
As the weather erratically switches
Between blinding light and grey shadows.
I sit with palms facing upwards
Enjoying the stillness and calm.
Intending to focus,
My thoughts run like a class of school children having
arrived at a play area;
Rounding them up, like a rancher, exhausts me.
I pause from my internal wrestling,
Choosing instead to breathe,
Notice what I can hear, and
Thank God for all the goodness
I see around me.
My rampant thoughts sit down
for an ice-cream and enjoy this
celebration of gratefulness.
The skies shift overhead.
The neighbours start drilling and sawing,
Which doesn't irritate me for once.
This church in my garden

Has become pure joy;
God and I look at each other,
Enjoying being present.
Peace floods my mind and
Electricity buzzes from my toes
To my crown.

HONESTY IS....

A glass of filtered water.

A pair of held-up, open palms.

Intimacy and vulnerability.

Easier when you trust each other.

Still a challenge if you're angry.

Not always right to give.

An open book.

Essential to my mental health.

STRIPPED AWAY

I want to only want to please you.
I know I often only please myself.

I only want to want to please you.
I want to lose my 'right' to self.

I want to want to please you, only.
I want myself to come second place.

I want only to want to please you.

<u>LISTEN CAREFULLY...</u>

Those who
Don't hear
The music,
Think the
Dancer is
Mad!

LOGOPHILE

I love the written word.

The roots, the stems, the buds

That flower into life.

I love the prefixes, suffixes,

Meanings, inferences and the ability

To project an idea onto your mind's surface.

That someone can see a picture,

MY mind conceived.

That I can get lost in entire worlds

Painted in words;

Narnia, The Shire, Space, Neverland, Wonderland and a
billion other places -

Real or imagined.

I love the utility of words;

Educating, informing, entertaining,

Instructing, persuading or complaining.

That they absorb the emotion

In poetry and prose that I digest

And feel too, like a Wonka-esque trick!

I love words' power.

They make me apprehensive

And can sting or burrow into my mind,

In ways more potent than when spoken.

I love that a note can change a day.

That hand-written letters can be a lifeline.

That a printed copy of Asterix, Tintin, The Beano or 'Oor Wullie' (in Scotland)

Can transport you to childhood hours

Desperate to stay awake.

I love finding new or long extinct words

The way Attenborough marvels at new

Creatures discovered.

I love learning about how society changed

With the advent of the printing press.

I love reading about 'Penny Dreadfuls'

And Dickens' stories sold in Victorian England.

I love how the written word can make

You cry-laugh or smile.

I love the curves, variety, spider marks and

Curls and idiosyncrasies of handwriting.

I.Love. The. Written. Word.

PEBBLE

One tiny, smooth, round, stone
In a shoe can eventually damage
And break someone,
Purely by its constant presence;
Its refusal to go anywhere.
Eventually, a human foot
Can become so blistered
And infected,
That in some cases
It needs to be amputated.
A pebble
Can do this!
Not by its size,
its mass, its power
Or its unique set of skills….
It breaks people down by
Its refusal to go anywhere;
Even while being repeatedly
Stepped on
And crushed.

A PRAISE PSALM BY ME.

The Lord is my strength and song;
Why should I be afraid?

He commands the rains to fall
and the sun to cast its light.
He answers my prayers and
stills my restless soul.

He sets the stars and planets in space.
All that is beautiful in nature points to him.
He accepted me despite myself.
All my past and wrongs were forgiven.

He commands the seas, land and air;
He created the mountains and all things, even down to the
tiniest quark.
He soothed my searching heart.
He gave me a hope I'd long forgotten.

The Lord is my strength and song;
Why should I be afraid?

I WISH. I WISH. I WISH.

I wish I could've saved you from
That mental breakdown;
You were living on your own
And we hadn't been in touch for a few years.

I wish I could've saved you from
That husband who cheated;
You always knew I wasn't keen on him
But I'm sorry that I let that put space
Between us.

I wish I could've saved you from
Those people who stabbed you in the back;
Who left you struggling to trust and
Believing the world was a less reliable place;
We'd lost touch and I never knew.

I wish I could've listened when you
Were the victim of domestic abuse;
I was wrapped up in myself and we
Only spoke once a year.
I wish we were close when you considered (then tried)
ending it all;
I wish you'd told me before you went for the

Cancer diagnosis appointment, rather than go on your own.

I wish. I wish. I wish. I wish. I wish. I wish.

I wish I'd realised sooner how precious old friends are;
I wish I'd told you about my own struggles too.

A PRAYER THE DAY AFTER I BECAME A CHRISTIAN

Dear God, please help me learn more and understand how to be a Christian.

Please help Laura understand and question.

Please help me be more like you as an example to my kids.

Please help my anger and old habits of pride, impatience and swearing.

Please help me quit smoking.

Please help us, as a family, find a church that we can be part of, serve and that can teach and support us.

Thank you for all you've started to do; for forgiving me and for never giving up on me.

Calum

'SUSURRUS' - (A 19TH CENTURY WORD, RARELY USED ANYMORE)

The low, soft, whispering of the trees
In a summer breeze.

A SALES PITCH FOR 1ST CENTURY CHRISTIANITY (AND BEYOND)

Roll up, roll up;

Gather round, gather round.

Join the followers of

'The Way';

You'll be rejected by your families,

Spat on, thrown in jail

And publicly beaten.

Our two leaders are:

1.A former Jewish religious leader

Who used to kill followers of 'The Way'

AND

2.An uneducated, hot-head, who

Used to be a fisherman.

Roll up, roll up.

Come one, come all.

You'll be laughed at, rejected

And despised.

In being known as a follower of

The Way and Jesus;

You'll face

Such possible deaths as crucifixion,

Stoning and being thrown into the arena

To be brutally killed by wild animals

Or gladiators.

You'll be buried in unmarked graves

(Or none at all) and the main tasks are

Telling others about Jesus, praying for and Serving others.

Roll up, roll up.

Gather round, gather round.

For the entire time you follow The Way,

People will plot to kill you,

spread lies about you and

Then accuse YOU of lying.

You are expected, if truly repentant,

To prioritise God before your self, family or friends.

You are expected to love your enemies

And love your neighbours as yourself.

You also accept that you forfeit security,

Safety and possessions,

when called to do so.

Roll up, roll up.

Come one. Come all.

WHEN GOD INTERVENES...

Shepherds become kings.

Swindlers become charitable.

Fishermen become leaders.

Cowards become courageous.

Prisoners become rulers.

Hateful people love their enemies.

Old, fragile, men and women birth nations.

Broken people bring healing to others.

Persecutors of Christians become church leaders.

'Fickle and faithless' become 'faithful and fearless'.

Prodigal, rebellious, runaways become welcomed, loved children; home and safe.

Weak become strong (in God's strength)

Divisive people become peacemakers.

Prostitutes become evangelists.

The anxious receive peace.

The blind see clearly.

Those living in darkness

receive (and shine) true light.

The lost are found.

WHAT DOES GOD LOOK LIKE?

'People say how can you know God if you can't see him? We don't even know what he looks like!!'

He walked the earth two- thousand years ago; everything he did was to show us who God was. In four 'gospels' written by Matthew, Mark, Luke and John we see the following portrait:

Empathy. A healer. Patience. A teacher. Power over the natural world. Power over any powers of darkness. Humility. Intelligence. Anger at injustice. Anger at hypocrisy and judgemental attitudes. Mercy. Someone who mixed with prostitutes and crooks; showing them love but instructing them to 'sin no more'.

Love. An encourager. He gave his followers responsibility, strength and power. He forgave, even when hurt by his closest friends. He was perfect, selfless and gentle. He was angered by injustice. He could do the impossible. Truth. Light. Wisdom.

Perceptive; seeing who people really were and who they could be. Social. He called people to him based on who HE was not based on who they were. He loved people regardless of gender, status or diseases. He gave, emptying himself again and again.

ALL he did was motivated by the desire to bridge the broken relationship we have with God. He loved to communicate what was on his heart. He instructed us to love God and love others before ourselves. He was fair. He was just.

This. Is the portrait of God I see in Jesus. This is what God looks like and so much more, having barely scratched the surface here.

If you want to know who God is, look at Jesus. He is the way, the truth and the life.

IT'S NOT...

It's not the hearing;
It's the understanding.
It's not the jumping off;
It's the landing.

It's not the fire;
It's the burning.
It's not the lecture;
It's the learning.

It's not the smile;
It's the glint.
It's not the question;
It's the hint.

It's not a law;
It's a fist.

It's not a poem;
It's just a list.

TONIGHT THERE WILL BE VIGILS AT THREE BRITISH UNIVERSITIES

I tried to end my life, the first time,

While aged eighteen and a half,

Away at Drama school…pre-university.

I was vulnerable. I was stuck in my head.

I didn't really talk much to my parents…

Or even my closest friends.

Today on the fourth of March twenty-twenty three, they will hold three vigils at universities in the United Kingdom;

Edinburgh, Bristol and London;

to highlight the increasing numbers who choose to end their own lives at uni.

Usually aged eighteen to twenty-one.

I wish I could share some magic formula

To help your kids or friends open up…

Or how to notice their inner battles,

Fighting the inner taunts repeatedly

Telling them *'kill yourself'*

'I wish I was dead.' or 'Would anyone care?'

When I attempted to end my life,

aged nineteen,

I was outgoing, sociable, constantly busy.

I had close friends of both genders.

I loved the course I was on…I was dating.

Anyone that knew me didn't think there was anything wrong. I hid my illness well.

There were no warnings, predictable signs.

or obvious clues…

In fact maybe there were a few…but

Only two or three people would have noticed

And they were neither family or lived in the same city as me.

I don't have any answers to protecting our beautiful, hopeful, aspirational, bright kids

(And friends) who are fighting invisible fights apart from this…

…Dare to be real and vulnerable *so*

Hopefully they will too.

Talk about mental health *without biased*

Labels or disdain.

Normalise talking to doctors when needing help and read up on things you're not sure about…please understand that even if you do all these things, it still mightn't be enough so make sure your kids or friends have information for charities like MIND and The Samaritans…

If you're Christians, pray for your kids daily AND make sure that your kids know that being a Christian doesn't mean you won't suffer mental illness…

It's ok to ask for help or see a doctor.

If away from home, at university, encourage them to join a church so they have a support network and Christian family to turn to.

People will remember loved ones and
Acquaintances tonight at three universities tonight
Because these young people thought their
Only option was to end their life…

What a waste. What loss. What pain they
Must have felt and struggled with.
Let's normalise talking about struggles.
Let's normalise talking about mental health.

Let's normalise encouraging each other to get the same help
we would suggest for physical illness.

DARLING IT'S BETTER DOWN WHERE IT'S WETTER; HOUSE PARTY UNDER THE SEA!

A tasseled Wobblegong watches; silent.

A Sarcastic Fringehead sighs at the

Dumbo Octopus dancing alone.

A peacock mantis shrimp has taken offence

At the Box Crab dancing with the Christmas Tree Worm he'd been eyeing up.

A Nudi Branch and Sea Angel have eaten

All the snacks on sticks so the Gulper Eel

Has nowt to gulp!

The Red-Lipped Batfish has incapacitated

A couple of thieving armoured snails trying to make a quick getaway.

A Vampire Squid and Flamingo Tongued snail are salivating at the guests - lecherous and hungry.

Coffinfish and Leafy Seadragons try cheering up a Blob Fish who was recently dumped…by a girl called Alice…down the loo!

Yeti Crabs, Jawfish and Goblin Sharks nip, bite and snap having had too much 'seaweed juice'; an Obese Dragonfish has been sent to turf them out.

Suddenly the music stops. Fights pause. Arguments halt as the familiar lights and sirens of the Angler Fish police appear on the horizon.

Creatures disappear, burrow into sand, head to the surface, change colour and groan as another party ends.

Sadly, it's back to school tomorrow.

HOODWINKED

Control was an illusion,
That reeled them in
And spat them out.

DECEIVED

Freedom was an illusion
That reeled them in
Then locked the door.

A RESTLESS, IMPATIENT SEASON - (JULY 2023)

One summer,

I woke up to find Autumn

In my garden and village.

It was tired of waiting for us

To discover it, to marvel at its

Colours, rain, wind and cool weather

So it turned up in July

Saying, dolefully,

'I waited for ages.

Where were you?!'

LOVE POEM (FOR MY WIFE)

You.

Only you.

My sun and moon.

You.

I AM STRUGGLING

I. Am. Struggling.

Today. Was. Tough.

I'm. Sick. Of. Pretending. I'm . O.K

Please. Will. Somebody. Notice. I'm. Not.

Please. Will. Somebody. Truly.

See. Me.

A PRAYER OF THANKS FOR FRIENDS

Dear God, thank you for friends…such as…

Friends we rarely see. Friends who understand. Online friends. Friends from school. Friends who were only in our lives for a wee while. Friends we can 100 percent be ourselves with. Friends who are honest with our best interests at heart. Friends who make us laugh. Friends that encourage us to do and be more. Friends who have become family. New friends.

Friends that know our worst sides and still love us. Friends who support us, even if they don't agree with us. Friends who we only see every few years, then when you do, time evaporates and it's as if we saw them yesterday.

Friends who have carried us. Friends who we've carried. Serious friends. Couple friends. Friends that died but left a profound impact on us. Close friends. Colleague friends. School run/playground, fellow parent friends. Friends who became *our* friends because they married our friends.

Friends who knew you while young and clueless - and the ones who are still your friends, now you're old(er) and still clueless. Friends forged from shared experiences- both good and bad. Friends who saved you by just being there. Friends who made you feel seen and valued; sometimes being the first people to do so.

Friends from the gym. Friends you met at uni, before cynicism or life hit hard. Friends you've spoken to all night until dawn. Friends you broke (minor) laws with. Friends that you call or text when you need advice or want to share good news.

Friends we only spent time with for a few days or weeks. Friends we've cried with. Friends who bought us food. Friends who encouraged us. Friends who were selfless. Friends who know all the best (and worst) stories about you. Friends who still call you by your teenage nickname.

Friends you have loads in common with. Friends who you don't have much in common with. Animal friends. Older friends. Younger friends. Friends who 'you can't remember how you became friends' friends. Friends you outgrew. Friends who you saw through. Friends who couldn't accept the new you, as you grew. Friends who have supported you. Friends who see loyalty and friendship as you do. Partners who became the best kind of friends, loving and accepting you.

Thank you God, for friends.

Calum x

THE PRICE OF SO-CALLED FREEDOM (EXODUS 12:33-14:14)

Moses, our 'great leader' had asked us to turn back a few nights ago, then set up camp by the water…before we knew it we heard thunder, shouting and clanking metal.

In the distance, through the dust and failing light we saw Pharaoh's army charging towards us, intent on either recapturing or wiping us out.

To the other side of us was the Red Sea. Did God bring us all this way to have us slaughtered or to drown ourselves. Moses, the arrogant idiot who challenged Pharaoh did this! For what?!!

They're getting nearer. My wife has started crying and my children are gripped to my waist asking 'what's happening Abba?' We have no way out. Maybe God is just another tyrant. Maybe all our sins have caught up with us.

Is it because there were no graves in Egypt that Moses brought us here to die? What has he done and why didn't he leave us alone, as we pleaded? It would have been better to keep serving the Egyptians than die in this dry, scorching, hopeless desert.

THe Egyptians are getting closer. A few brave people are picking up farming tools or daggers but it won't help. There are tears and holding and goodbyes and people saying they love each other; it might be the last time.

As for Moses? He's standing on a rock by the water shouting over the fear and panic and goodbyes saying we should walk towards the sea, while he raises his staff....

...He's telling us to trust God! The carts, donkeys and people are slowly moving. The ground is shaking with the force of the army nearly upon us, while Moses shouts 'Go!'

We're doomed. My children are crying now and God is nowhere to be seen...

WILD THINGS!

Let's stay up all night and be rock n roll;

We'll make toast and marmite,

Then drink cups of strong tea.

We'll watch '24 Hours in A + E',

Discussing Star Wars, Netflix and Books.

We'll play Spotify, while deciding to tidy the kitchen,

reciting all the lyrics we know,

That don't make sense…

Then decide that's enough frivolity for one night and drag ourselves to bed at

10.45 p.m, knowing that we rocked and rolled for a good three hours!

Next time we might even go crazy and make fresh, filter coffee and crumpets!

Heck yeah!!!

A PINK TUTU

My beautiful, giggling, blue eyed baby girl had returned from a weekend at her biological dad's...

...Crying, confused and tired after emotional abuse and a lack of routine had rattled her. *Again.*

To cheer her up, her big brother and I offered to do anything she wanted to cheer her up.

She answered so we left the room,

putting on our leotards and tutus as she led us through a dance class.

Laughing and doubling over on her bed,

she smiled the smile of

knowing she was safe, she was loved...

...and she was home.

TWO OPTIONS

Some of you reading this
Will one day die and
Receive a welcome in heaven
That will be far beyond
Your wildest dreams;
Having decided to follow Christ
In this life, accepting his forgiveness
And choosing to live for him.

Some of you reading this
Will one day die and enter a loneliness and separation
From God and anything else good
That will be far beyond
You worst nightmares;
Having decided to reject God's
Offer of forgiveness, love, And freedom...
In choosing to live your own way.

There are no other options. Whether you believe or not won't change the outcome; the choice is yours:

Accept God's love, forgiveness and grace or face the consequences of your unresolved sin.

LONGING TO BE ROAMIN' IN THE GLOAMIN'

(A nod to 'Home thoughts from abroad' by

Robert Browning)

Oh to be in Scotland,

Now that Summer's here...

Lying at night with a duvet.

Going to bed without fear

Of restless hours,

Still awake, in bed.

Sweltering days,

When your face is red.

Of cloud bathing days,

While the sky is grey.

A haggis supper

Before making hay.

A rain shower or storm

Coming doon

In every way.

The days are getting hotter

And cranking up a gear...

Oh to be in Scotland,

Now that Summer's here.

'A FEW GOOD MEN' (FROM YORKSHIRE) BECOME DENTISTS...

Him - I want t' tooth!!!

T'other- You want t' tooth?

Him - I want t' tooth.

T'other - You can't handle t' tooth!

Him - I think I'm entitled.

BREATHLESS

I left the house shivering,
While frozen grass
crunched beneath my feet;
I shielded my eyes,
Blinded by the reflected light
On frost-dusted trees, cars and windows.
Breathing heavily,
I struggled to catch my breath;
Walking and slipping,
I eventually caught up with it.
Holding it like a frozen bubble
In my hands, I popped it then sucked in
The warm, moist air;
Drinking in loss and light and
Life.

CHRISTIANITY IS HATED BECAUSE IT IS TRUE...

Christianity tells you the truth
About everything:

It tells you the truth about God,
The truth about humanity.
The truth about time.
The truth about eternity.
The truth about heaven.
It's the truth about Hell,
Truth about life,
Truth about death.
Truth about sin.
The truth about righteousness.
The truth about creation,
The truth about consummation.

It's the truth because
The Bible is the truth.
Make no mistake,
There is such a being asThe Devil
and he is known as
'The father of lies'.
He is a liar
Who works to convince the world

Of those lies.

He is at war with God,

At war with Christ,

At war with The Holy Spirit.

At war with The Bible.

At war with the Gospel.

At war with the church.

(Adapted from a John MacArthur sermon)

LOST (FOR LAURA, MY WIFE)

I'm marooned on an island

That's the black pupil of your eye

Surrounded by a sea of green and ochre.

Permanently lost and abandoned there

Since my world crash landed into yours and I was castaway…

…on a Friday.

MY SONS APPROACH THE AGE OF THIRTEEN

I feel torn between wanting to
Push you to discover snd explore;
And *not* wanting you to grow up.
I fight the urge to keep you safe,
While understanding you need risk
To teach you how to keep yourself safe.
I want you here, with us,
And I'm not sure I'm ready to let go.

Please be patient with me son-
I worry.

Love Dad x

GOING UP

BMI,
Cholesterol,
Electricity
And gas prices
But not
My
Height

DADS WHO LOVE TO HELP

My children often choose not
To tell us about something
They're worried about or
Something that's hurting…
It breaks my heart because
They don't need to 'go it alone'
And I want to help;
In fact I love helping them
Because they're my kids.
I realised today that
I often do the same with
My own Heavenly Father.
I keep worries to myself and
Try to go it alone,
While he, the perfect Dad,
Wants to help and listen
Because he loves me.

SLEEPER

I remember my first time travelling on a
Sleeper train - wrapped in a scratchy, heavy, blanket,
Being rocked by the soothing

'Rackety-clack, rackety clack'

And gentle swaying.
I left the window slightly open
So I could hear every sound
And breathe in every foreign smell,
While we travelled from Harare, Zimbabwe
To our destination, in the mountains.

Like a sponge, I soaked up voices; as we stopped at stations
with nose-tingling smells of grilled meat and engine oil;
While my soft, plush pillow, made the fight
To stay awake a losing battle.
I woke every hour or so, through the night;

'Rackety-clack, rackety-clack'
Listening and inhaling the countryside
So I could recall this night, in decades to come...
It was the best night's sleep of my life
And one of my favourite journeys...

Aged twenty; full of wonder
And the desire to smell, hear and taste, the
Unfamiliar and new.

Rackety-clack
Rackety-clack
Rackety-clack
Rackety-clack

PLEASE DON'T BE AFRAID TO STAND OUT! (FOR MY FOUR KIDS)

Be a rainbow coloured lamb
in a field of white sheep.
When everyone wants to party,
Have a sleep.
If everyone's raving to a dance DJ thrum,
Say stuff it and move to the beat
Of your own drum.
If everyone thinks you should fight fire with fire,
Mix it up and calm it with water on the pyre.
If everyone thinks that bright fashion is dead,
Dress like you're born to stand out; wear red.
If everyone's swimming in a clockwise direction,
Decide to go 'anti' you might provoke reflection.
If everyone's chasing the same illegal highs,
Be the one to have a cuppa, sit in silence, ignore the sighs.
When the world says *'you should be'* say *'No way! I'll decide…'*
When the world says to blend in don't disappear or hide.
When the world says you might be seen as strange or odd,
Show them you're proud and not a 'needy bod'.
If the worker ants question while they look and act the same,
If the buzzy bees grumble you're not playing the game,
If the flies flying around look down because you're walking,

Then you're doing something right, if it's about you they're talking.

You're born to excel, dance, jump and take flight.

You're born to make a path to what YOU know is right,

One day these people won't even be in sight,

So stand tall, be a rainbow and share your light...

...Just give me a call if you need me.

Sleep Tight!

Love Dad x

BUT GOD...

I nearly succeeded aged 19, when I tried
To kill myself...but God.

I couldn't trust anyone...but God...

I am flawed, imperfect and still struggle with
Different things...but God...

Phone calls and talking to new people were
Impossible for me...but God...

My wife and I nearly divorced last year...but God.

I was full of anger and irritability and impatience...but God.
I was full of hurt, trauma, un-forgiveness
And hatred...but God

I nearly became an alcoholic...but God

Several times I nearly took a knife to someone...but God...

I was weighed down by guilt and anxiety
And the pointlessness of life...but God...

I was selfish and only looked after myself
And my family…but God…

I tried reading all kinds of books on
Philosophy, religions, psychology…but God…

…But God. But God. But God. But God…

This time last year I wanted to die…
…But God…

Written September 2023

DON'T BE AFRAID

In the Bible Jesus or angels say
'Do not fear' or 'don't be afraid'
Approximately one hundred and forty five times…

…in other forms the idea is expressed
Three hundred and sixty five times;

As though God knew his creation so well
That he would have to remind us every day of the year to
'fear not';

that fear shouldn't be the driving force
Of our lives…

That if we trust God,

His perfect love will cast out ALL
Fear.

MY WIFE CHECKS IN WITH ME...

I've been finding some things a challenge;
Knowing that I had to deal with something today, she asked me:

'How did you find this morning?'

I quickly replied:

'Well, I came downstairs...and there it was.'

Cue hysterical giggling...sat on the floor...wiping our eyes.

MY FIRST ATTEMPT AT PRAYING

I mumbled and fumbled through an
Awkward conversation with God.
Some might call it a prayer but two
Seconds in I was already apologising
For swearing…
To a God I wasn't sure was real.
My prayer was simply this:

'Please help me understand,
If you are real.
Please help me with the many questions
And 'learning' I've had
That conflicts
With the Christian faith.
Please help me know.'

As I came to the door of my house
One, long forgotten, verse of scripture
Sprung to mind:

'Be still and know that I am God.'

So maybe I'd start with that.

SOCK 'N' ROLL

At midnight the socks, are woken by clocks

And meet by the washing machine.

They all come in pairs; no graces or heirs

In a crowd of both dirty and clean.

The queen of the socks, checks the doors and the locks,

Before calling the mumbles to hear…

With a twinkle of glee, she will soon set them free,

To run, hide and disappear.

The nightly game of hide and seek

Is what all socks love doing each night;

Whether old, new or smelly, rolled up in some wellies,

This is their nightly delight.

They scatter and scarper, scamper and flee

Until caught when they sit for a chat,

Taking turns to be seeker,

the dark starts to get weaker;

The sun rises and well, that's that.

Wherever the socks are when sunrise starts

Is where they will remain for the day,

Under fridges, or cupboards or on doors or stairs until the next evening of fun and play.

TEMPERATURE GAUGE

A thermometer changes, according to the temperature and atmosphere of the room or environment it's in.

A thermostat changes the temperature and atmosphere of the room (or environment) it's in.

If you're a Christian, God did not call us to be thermometers-he made us to be, in his strength,

thermostats.

COLD AND DISTANT

Crashing lows roll over me

Like determined, crushing waves.

I know God's there.

I know the Bible is true.

I know Christ died for me and rose again

But there's a numbness…

A spiritual indigestion.

I've confessed my sin.

I read the Bible daily.

I pray…

And yet still, God seems so far away.

My ears are muffled.

My patience is fraying.

My peace, threadbare…

My heart feels cold.

HOPE (FOR MY ELDEST DAUGHTER)

A sparkle,

a rainbow,

a grin,

a hand held,

a giggle,

a cuddle,

a drawing,

a reader,

a baby;

An instant love.

My Hope.

POINT SCORING

Sometimes,
When you lose
You win
And sometimes
When you win,
You lose.

WHAT IS THE POET'S PURPOSE?

Maybe our role is to hold a mirror

To the sun and reflect it elsewhere.

Maybe it's to look closely at the tiny details

Then show you what we've found.

Maybe it's to be a prism of light shining different hues you might not see.

Maybe it's to pull apart the stitches of old wounds so you can see others hurt too.

Maybe it's to show you old scars so you can believe that survival is possible.

Maybe it's because we simply have to send the words tumbling out of us somewhere.

Maybe it's just to build or create something that wasn't there before.

Maybe it's to satirise and surprise so you laugh or smile when life's hard.

Maybe it's to help you feel less alone because others have felt the same.

Maybe it's to jolt you awake to a realisation you needed to see.

Maybe it's a form of therapy…for the author; maybe it's just for me.

AN ODE TO BRITPOP

I scratch me Elbow and release a

Primal Scream.

I go down stairs, make my orange juice;

Squeezing the Pulp, then put on me

Suede jacket.

I meet me mates for lunch, giving them an

Embrace…

My lunch is a bit Dodgy, so I have a can of Black Grape. I think it was off because the afternoon goes by in a Blur.

I reported those Charlatans at the cafe because I'm a Supergrass.

After a sleep, I made a Lush smoothie with some Lightning Seeds, which sorted me out.

I smoked a cigarette, watching the Ash

fall on a Babybird.

Walking to the Cornershop, I decided to buy some Shampoo and Super Furry Animals;

I put all my new items in Shed Seven and

I went home, had a nap and dreamed of being in a beautiful, hot, Oasis.

I WON'T WAIT (A NOD TO JENNY JOSEPH)

I don't want to wait until I'm older
To wear purple.
For too long I've hidden under
'Blend in' colours of black or grey.
For too long I've forgotten
The colours of who I am.
I've mistakenly wrapped myself
In the safety of black jackets,
T-shirts of muted colours
And inoffensive cuts or hues.
No more.
I do not want to promise myself
That I will wear purple when I'm older.
I want to robe myself in rainbows
Of stand-out, love-or-hate shades
That state
I am here.
I have something to say
See me.

'HELLO OLD FRIEND...'

Is how I like to greet my oldest, most special friends that have known me longest;

who often only call me by an abbreviation or nickname.

I stole the greeting from X-Men where either Ian McKellan or Patrick Stewart say it to each other in their well-spoken, rich, timbre.

It's a greeting that recognises that despite having lived in 35 houses; 16 towns, villages or cities; I still have a history made of people I'm privileged to know.

It recognises the few people that always accepted me as I was,

without ridicule or bullying;

the people who became the family

I chose.

It focuses on the passing of time where age, distance and circumstances haven't changed a bond that I still cherish,

so if in years to come I greet you with

'hello old friend' please see it as the compliment it's meant to be.

NAMES FOR SNOW THAT MY PHONE DOESN'T ACCEPT ARE REAL:

Sposh, blizzard, onding, skift, graupel, grue, corn-snow, sleet, lumi, myuki, nivia, yukina, edur, fannar, nas, tuhin, yukio, zane, chan, eira, flykra, haukea, flindrikin, skovin, drift, snaw, snowpocalypse, pow-pow, snizzle, snice, tuyet, earth-dandruff, pauxder, funter, snuee, smirr, feefle, snaw-pouther, skirlie, skiftin, snaw-bree, clag, brak, sneepa, tirl, haar-frost, feuchter, smeuk, wauff,

FRAGILE

Have you ever thought about how
Vulnerable a human baby is;
How utterly fragile, dependant and
Weak they are.
Other animals stand instantly,
Able to run.
Many are born with teeth, claws or
Thick skin…but human babies?!!
Thin, fragile skin and bones;
A skull that isn't completely fused together.
No teeth or claws.
No ability to run, stand or even crawl away.
If a soldier tried to kill them with swords,
They could easily.
If a wild animal or older child wanted to
Hurt them, they could.
Everything about being a human baby is
Fragile, dependant, vulnerable and weak.
This………..this is who God became;
All powerful, all knowing, God
Who created the earth, the universe and us
Became fragile, dependant, vulnerable and
Weak.
Why would an almighty bring choose to

Willingly do that? To be fully human?

Maybe it's because he loved us

And wanted us to know what he was like?!

Maybe it's because sin always has a price,

Which was paid for in full, when that frail baby grew up and chose to die in our place.

IS IT ME YOU'RE LOOKING FOR?

I woke up, checked my phone:

Facebook, Instagram, TikTok, LinkedIn, Sky News, The weather, WhatsApp, Twitter, Messenger and Sky Sports.

Got dressed.

Read the morning's Bible reading on my phone, while I had a long wee.

Had my breakfast. Sorted the kids. Then off to work until morning coffee break:

Facebook, Instagram, TikTok, LinkedIn, Sky News, The weather, WhatsApp, Twitter, Messenger and Sky Sports.

More work.

Lunch - I sat with my mates but I didn't join in with the gossip....Debbie's fella sounds a nightmare though and how immoral is our department boss sleeping with....well, you know....

More work.

Afternoon coffee:

Facebook, Instagram, TikTok, LinkedIn, Sky News, The weather, WhatsApp, Twitter, Messenger and Sky Sports.

Home.

Checked phone:

Facebook, Instagram, TikTok, LinkedIn, Sky News, The weather, WhatsApp, Twitter, Messenger and Sky Sports.

Made dinner. Chatted with the kids.

Phoned my parents.

Checked phone:

Facebook, Instagram, TikTok, LinkedIn, Sky News, The weather, WhatsApp, Twitter, Messenger and Sky Sports.

Watched Netflix.

Bed.

Checked phone:

Facebook, Instagram, TikTok, LinkedIn, Sky News, The weather, WhatsApp, Twitter, Messenger and Sky Sports.

Evening prayer time, where I shared my frustration that I just don't feel like you speak to me....are you still there God?

Hello?

CHILDREN OF WAR

The children of war
Wear crowns on their heads
Made of used bandages
That have bullet-hole,
Blood-seeped poppies
Arranged intermittently.
The children of war
Have eyes that constantly search
The distance for a returning
Family member.
Eyes that rake the skies
And feverishly gorge on words
Within books…while shells fall.
The children of war crave home;
Not a house or a three bed semi
But the home where language
Doesn't rattle in unfamiliar heavy fire.
Home, where smells on the street
Make promises of mum's cooking.
The children of war triple check doors,
Hold hammers under pillows and
always sleep one ear open while they sleep,
As the world looks the other way.
Children of war learn to pretend

Not to understand the vitriol thrown

In stares, comments and mutters of

'Go back to where you came from'

The children of war can't go back to

A house, city or home that is so disfigured,

The media drapes a shroud over it

So no one has to look at it.

The children of war look for reassurance

From parents, that look away because they can't guarantee safety.

The children of war are the victims of theft;

Their innocence, their rights;

their chance to grow and love and age -

In the country which is fused to their bones.

The children of war's roots have been

Poisoned,

Yet they dig deeper, looking for a home they may never

See again.

TRUTH (WRITTEN SEPTEMBER 2022)

See you can argue apologetics

Or say my Bible isn't true;

There's one thing

You simply can't do…

You can't say that my years

Of feeling angry weren't real.

You can't say that I didn't have

Wounds needing to heal.

You can't say that my mental health

Nearly led me to my death.

You can't say I didn't hate myself

With every fibre or breath.

That despite things I achieved,

There was still unsatisfaction.

That my self-control or peace

Weren't permanently in traction.

This is a fraction

Of the life I've lived since I was twenty.

Have I seen much of life?

Believe me I've seen plenty.

The sex left me empty.

My career, full of dread.

None of them silenced

The destruction in my head.

As I've said, you can't say

That the end wouldnt call and taunt.

That all of the booze

From my favourite haunts,

Only stilled me for an hour or

Maybe a few.

You can't say that wasn't real

But I can tell you…

I can tell you when I asked God

To hear me; he did.

He'd been waiting,

He still loved me.

I was still his kid.

Though I hid. He waited.

Then opened my eyes to see and

In the past four weeks…

I feel free.

JUNE PRAYER

Dear God,

Please be near to my friends who are lonely, exhausted, in pain or who feel lost.

Please reveal yourself to them if they ask you to help them understand and know you.

Please bring peace to their homes, marriages and relationships.

Thank you for your patience, love and forgiveness.

May my friends understand and see how good and loving you are.

Calum

TAPESTRY

If you look at the back of a tapestry

It's a disorganised, scruffy, occasionally pretty (but nonsensical) mess.

Threads cross over. Others head nowhere.

Some snap. Others are tied off.

Some, stand, scruffily frayed.

The picture is not clear.

There isn't even the hope of possible clarity.

In six months of being a Christian

I've realised that a lot of things in life

Look like the back of that tapestry...

With a healthy dose of worry or panic

Thrown in.

It's only in God's timing and purposes

That he shows us what he's been doing;

That the mess and scruffiness and threads going nowhere, were actually being directed

By the master craftsman...

God knows what he's doing. God loves you. God is in control; and if you trust him he'll eventually show you the full picture. He'll show you the purpose in your pain.

FATHER OF LIES

He deals in the false, half-truths and things
You believe are true but aren't.
His nature is to reproduce and birth lies;
Lies that keep you searching for love,
Acceptance, peace and purpose
In all the wrong places;
Better still, you'll think that all of these
Explorings and discoverings are your ideas;
That you're 'self-actualising',
Exercising your freedom
And that you'd never believe blatant lies…
See the Devil uses pride, doubt and
Flawed logic to support his lies but
As a famous film once said:
'The greatest trick the Devil pulled was
Convincing the world he doesn't exist.'
We're so wrapped up in thinking *we're*
The only, most supreme beings in the world
That it's easier to point to other humans
Being responsible for the epitaphs, shame
And distracting poison that sits in our minds, driving us.
We laugh at suggestions some evil being
Would be orchestrating these things
For some nefarious purposes…

We prattle and rattle on
While he laughs ecstatically,
Dripping more poison in your ear.
His only; one and only aim is this:
That you would be separated from God
In this life and for eternity.
That you would suffer, die and experience
Pain because you remind him of your Heavenly Father.
He will use lies to make sure you
Go nowhere near God and convince you
It's all from your intelligent, reasoned logic.
He knows full-well that on the cross
Jesus defeated him once and for all.
He knows all powers have been placed
Under Jesus' feet.
That when Jesus roared 'it is finished'
On the cross - it was.
He knows that Jesus is 'the way, the truth
And the life',
So he'll do anything to keep you from
Seeing that truth.
Wake up and see you've been had.

We all were.

It's never too late to see the truth and get right with God.

INQUIRE

Ask, research, investigate, critique, analyse, look, see, explore, find, discover, weigh-up-evidence, find-multiple-sources; look at individual experiences from a wide demographic; read writings from different eras, question without agenda or bias...

...The evidence for God and his Word (The Bible) can (*and will*) withstand the scrutiny.

Just please, look into it and inquire; your present (and, more importantly, your future) depends on it.

CHAINED (ACTS 12:5-17)

A thin strip of light lay on the cell floor,

The only visible ray of hope.

He knew his brothers and sisters were praying so he got down on his knees and

Began praising God for his provision,

Even though he was chained between two soldiers.

He started reciting the psalms of David, while the soldiers hit him and spat on him,

Wine soaked saliva soaking his beard.

'Where is this God?' 'Where is he?',

They sneered.

Several hours later, he lay beaten, asleep;

Having had his tunic pulled from him.

His wrists were bleeding, still chained

To the two Roman soldiers.

A blinding flash knocked the guards from their feet, as the chains fell off his wrists.

Hitting him on the side, the helper said:

'Arise quickly. Get ready, tie your sandals, put your tunic on and follow me.'

He walked past the first set of cells;

Guards slumped unconscious against the walls, to the outer courtyard and main gates- guards collapsed; swords sheathed.

They went down a near side street

And as he turned to ask something,

The visitor had gone.

He went straight to the house of his

Brothers and sisters, who had been

Praying through the night.

A little girl, not knowing who he was,

Left him standing outside while she told

The group of believers that someone called

'Peter' was outside.

They spent the remaining two hours of night

Praising God, laughing, eating and praying for others still in chains.

YOU WERE ON HIS MIND

My Lord, my friend, my saviour
Hung on a cross;
Nails driven through his wrists
And a rusted, metal spike hammered
Through his feet.
As his body strained for breath,
Having to lever himself though
His impaled feet, to take a breath,
He looked below;
Soldiers shouting abuse at him,
Mocking him to save himself
If he was God.
Other soldiers divided his clothes,
Gambling to win the bounty
As blood streaked down my saviour's face;
Looking at the religious leaders,
Smiling at his downfall, the soldiers laughing, the criminal
beside him hurling abuse and the billions of people that
would
Mock, ignore and insult him in years to come,
He cried out to God
on their (and our) behalf saying:
'Father forgive them, for they know not what they do.'
That my Lord thought about me

On that cross while he was dying;

That he would pray for the people

Who's sin or actions held him there

Because he knew it was the only way

We could be saved…

He cried out to God to forgive us

Because we didn't realise what we were doing because if we
understood just a fraction of what he'd done for us,

We would fall to our knees,

Beg for forgiveness and offer nothing else

But our lives, as a tiny expression of our

Thanks.

REDEEMED

I'm old but I'm bold
Heart no longer cold.
My life has been bought
With his blood -
I'm sold.
I was bought at a price.
I was cleansed of my sin.
A new year dawns.
Let's live for Christ.
Let's begin.

20/20

I think that when we think about God,
It's like a 'magic eye' picture;
You have to look beyond the mess of
Some aspects of organised religion
Or mistakes and atrocities that have been done, Wrongly,
in the name of God;

If you want to see the real message
And personality of God,
Look at Jesus in the gospels who preached
Love, forgiveness, peace and asked people to follow him;
How he acted in a counter-cultural way
To include women,
despite their low status in Middle Eastern society;

When that image becomes clearer you'll see
Selflessness, sacrifice, anger at injustice
And a desire that all would follow him;
You'll see him standing up to the establishment, religious
leaders and above all, compassion.

If you're ever tempted to consider
God being the total some of
Your views on aspects of organised religion

Or the failings of humans,

Try and see God, who became human,

Who came to sacrifice his own life

Because he loved more selflessly than anyone.

I ASK THEM TO TAKE A POEM....

and 'hold it up to the light'; listen to its heartbeat 'ba-bum ba-bum ba-bum'

I ask them to sit in a room with only the poem, listening to the pauses and rests between words.

I ask them to put it in a 'proving drawer', then leave it to rise, before working and kneading it.

I ask them to dissect it, flip it, deconstruct it and then plant it in a pot full of Scrabble tiles.

I ask them to bleed on it, whisper to it; then wait until it reveals its truths.

CARRIED ALONG BY A ROSE-BUD

My wee rose-bud youngest,
Came with me as I did the rounds
Of library and shop...
I hadn't been out the house in two weeks
Due to my agoraphobia
So I tried to keep my shaking hands
Under control, as her tiny,
Seven-year-old hand gripped my mine.

She pointed out a large, rose petal
(That I'd usually have missed,
In the rush of getting home
As quickly as possible)
We debated and wondered if it was pink
Or peach...or red...or a blend...
We discussed the shape and size...
'The rose must've been ginormous';

Which then led to us discussing our
Favourite smells and flowers.
Without realising it, we were outside
Our tiny, village, library...
Conversations of nature and favourites
Having carried us along;

Just enjoying each other's company.
I looked down at my hand.

It wasn't shaking…
So we walked back -
Slowly.

COMMUNITY

Imagine a church where

They choose to meet daily;

Out of excitement and community.

A church where people

sell their possessions (*and property)*

To provide for fellow believers in need.

Imagine a church where

People's joy radiates from them

And they constantly pray and praise God.

A church where people

Are unified in a common goal,

That supersedes any disagreements.

Imagine a church where

People share food, things they've learned from the bible and their struggles, daily.

A church where people truly follow the Bible's example…

No one could fail to notice and be drawn to that.

ADVICE TO 'THE COMMON PEOPLE'

'The poor should learn to shop and
Cook properly!'
Was said in parliament last week,
By a politician representing
'The people'....
Well I've trawled my budget cookbooks
And budget recipe websites but
Nothing was magically solved...
So I came up with a recipe you could
Relay to parliament for me:
Let's take all the darkness in houses
That can't afford to switch lights on
And put it in a bowl.
Then stir in some division about Brexit,
The Environment and 'the haves versus
The have-nots'.
Take a handful of reduced products from
The reduced aisles - it doesn't matter if the ingredients don't
go together...
Add a few cookery lessons learning to
Cook with bread and jam or beans on toast
Fifty different ways...or some lessons on
'How to get your daily amount of calories in one meal'
Throw in a few handfuls of foods you can

Cook without needing to use the gas

Or electric.

Don't forget to season with a government

Who partied, while people died alone during a pandemic.

Then take all these elements and see if YOU

Can create something *you* can stomach.

'SLOW IT DOWN'

Slow dancing with you
At 12.15 a.m,
Playing you my favourite
Lumineers' song;
We kiss furtively,
Stroke each others' faces
And smile like teenagers
Having their first dance together…

PARADISE

It's

Not a place on earth-

(Stay anywhere long enough

And it loses its sheen...)

But sat with you

And our bonnie bairns

On Christmas Eve

Watching a movie,

with steaming, hot chocolate,

Is pretty bloomin'

Close.

WHAT ABOUT THE CLEANERS?

Who cleans the school
After another mass shooting?
Who scrubs blood splatters from
The wipeable board as black, red
And white mix in the
squeezed sponge-water?

Who scoops up fragments of brain,
Bone and intestines into a yellow tub?
Who mops, brushes, sanitises and polishes,
While salty tears and heaving shoulders,
Crumple under the weight of minimum
Wage?!

Do A-graded tests get binned because
They're stamped with a single droplet
Of blood?

What about displays that showcase the work of a low ability
kid whose work was chosen as they tried really hard but
there's pieces of skull on it now?!
Do chairs, tables and boxes of coloured pencils get burned or
sent to the dump so everyone can forget that this equation

Doesn't add up...the right to own guns doesn't make children safer!

When the class room is clean and sterile, smelling of bleach, who cleans the minds of the cleaners? Who scrubs the trauma from the students and staff that walk by that classroom daily?

Who cleans a country of damaging, dangerous, outdated 'rights' that were decided hundreds of years ago?

MAY 2022 PRAYER

Dear God,

Please be near to my Christian brothers and sisters in the Middle East.

May you protect them and give them strength in difficult, heart sapping circumstances.

Please listen to them, as they cry for peace and opportunities to show others your love.

May you show them your direction as they live by your word and honour you with their lives.

Please give them the strength to keep persevering and the strength to love others, as you love us.

Thank you for your goodness and your protection for these brave brothers and sisters.

Amen

(I wrote this after reading the book 'Light Force' by Brother Andrew)

EX-TEACHER, OVER 40, FEELS LOST (WRITTEN IN 2019)

Lost at sea
No vocation
Loss of identity situation.
I struggle to admit
My career has gone.
If what I am, is what I do
Then this feels wrong.
Alone in a desert;
Trapped down a mine.
Feeling claustrophobic in
the unemployment line.
I struggle to admit
My career is gone.
If what I am, is what I do,
Then what's gone wrong?!

WHAT DOES LOVE LOOK LIKE?

Look at Jesus on that cross.

Look at his bleeding, bruised body.

Really look at his open gashes and wounds;

At the rusted, nails piercing sinew and bone.

Look at Jesus writhing in agony.

Look at him strain to take in one breath.

Really look at the the thorns pressed into his head;

At the mocking sign above him saying

'King of the Jews'

Look at Jesus, barely clothed and exposed.

Look at the bones visible through deep cuts.

Really look at his broken, cut, bruised face;

At that face while blood, tears and sweat mingle and drip down.

Look at Jesus dying slowly, spluttering blood.

Look at his side pierced, roughly, by a spear.

Really look at him stuttering and muttering prayers;

At his pained eyes, full of compassion before a final, guttural roar of:

'It. Is. Finished.'

RAIN

Rods

Cats

dogs

Sheets

spray

Fine

Cold

Warm

Sleety

Torrential

For days

For seconds

Forever

For quiet

For survival

Sopping

Soaked

Dripping

Bloomin' torrential,

Wonderfully

British,

Rain!

GUESSING GAME...

(Forgotten statistics)

At least 130,000

Maybe 220,000

Possibly 500,000

Tangibly 800,000

At worst 1,500,000

Of the estimated **1-2 Million**

Roma and Sinti people who were

Ethnically cleansed

(As though they were

Dirt and grime)

During *World War* Two.

(My great grandparents were travellers, of Roma heritage.)

PEP TALK FOR CHRISTIANS GOING THROUGH IT...

Let me assure you and remind you
To see how big God is.
Please let me ask you to pause;
Resting in how much God loves you
And how infinitely mighty he is.
His love for you knows no bounds.
His compassion for you is limitless.
His heart breaks when you
Strain and haul at huge loads
Of worries, cares and struggles
That you've already prayed about.
See he loves it when you bring
Even the most seemingly insignificant
Worry to him; he is the perfect Dad.
He loves answering prayers;
When you rely on his strength.
He is completely sovereign,
Which means nothing is beyond
His control.
If you are facing darkness, challenges,
Sickness, fears about the future or
Are struggling to understand where God is -
Please bring it to him.

Talk to him about it.

Praise him for the fact that his love, truth,

Mercy and forgiveness never change.

Praise him for ALL the times he's

Answered prayers and surprised you.

Know that 'he who began a good work

In you will see it through to completion'.

It's easy-er to trust and speak of God's

Goodness when times are peaceful.

It's easier to bounce along worry-free

When you're on level, calm, ground...

But God loves you too much to

Leave you the way you are;

He sees the whole picture.

He sees the victory and the celebration.

He's heard your cries and desire

To be more like Jesus; it makes him smile.

BUT to answer those heart-longings;

To move you forward; to help you grow up,

This is what you need to endure.

He sees the future testimony.

He sees the person you're becoming and

He loves you more than you can ever

Comprehend.

He never promised you would never have trouble in this
world but he did say:

'Take heart, I have overcome the world.'

Lean into his loving arms and remember,

As you lean into him,

When you are weak, then you are strong and it might be you
that is needed to tell

Someone else this, when you're through it.

WHY?

Why do people criticise Christianity, citing conflicts that happened under the guise of faith BUT don't mention the 110 million people that died under atheists such as Lenin, Stalin, Mao, Pol Pot.

Why do people talk about hypocrites (which exist in all walks of life) but never the charities started by Christians; or the work done with the poor and needy in God's name?

Why do people demand 100% proof of God without realising the theories of evolution or the Big Bang are nowhere near 100% provable...and never will be?

Why do people speak of Christians being 'brainwashed', 'having Stockholm syndrome' and 'cognitive dissonance' without seeing that the same can be said about what the world's told them?

COUNTER-CULTURE

Let's love our enemies and
Pray for those who attack us.
Let's lend, without expectations
And when someone asks for our top;
Let's offer them our coat too.
Let's love our neighbours, community
And friends,
As much as we love ourselves.
Let's forgive, even when people aren't sorry.
Let's forgive when the wound still hurts.
Let's give and never get tired
In giving.
Let's serve, without expecting praise,
Thanks or even 'returned favours'.
Let's turn the other cheek.
Let's be there for the wounded and lost.
Let's not just love our friends and family.
Let's share, while others hold tight.
Let's give while others accumulate.
Let's cry with others,
rather than being glad it's not us.
Let's feed the hungry.
Let's be a friend to those who have
Nothing to offer us in return.

Let's listen, without planning what WE
Want to say next.
Let's encourage rather than crave praise.
Let's celebrate others' successes.
Let's love and care for; let's see others'
Needs before our own....
Can you *imagine* a world where everyone
Did ALL these things?!!

GOD-INCIDENCES

When I've prayed about lacking something

And then *that day* received that thing;

Often from an unexpected source.

When I prayed for my friend's son who,

The following day, went to his physiotherapist,

Only to be told he was healing faster than expected.

When someone who hasn't slept well

For days, weeks and months does so

The day I started praying.

Appointments that have come through quickly, scans being found to be clear;

People finally being put on housing lists...

Prayers answered, which I haven't prayed about, only for God to seemingly say:

'I knew you needed this and more'.

My friends' prayers for me,

for twenty-two years, despite my passionate

Hatred of the Bible and God...

...Only to see me become a Christian.

In nine months of being a Christian

I have seen approximately 70 answers to prayer,

That some people would dismiss as pure coincidence...but...

...At what point does it go beyond the realm of statistical chance?

After the hundredth answer to prayer?

The five hundredth?

Maybe the thousandth?

God answers prayer.

God changes lives.

There is simply too much evidence
That backs it up.

WHAT ARE HEAVY? (A NOD TO CRISTINA ROSSETTI)

What are heavy? Regret and Autumn rain.

What are brief? Lives and pain.

What are frail? Young hearts and trust.

What are deep? Lost memories and dust.

NONSENSE COMMON-SENSE

I'm bing bong bananas,

Trippy dippy doo!

I'm boodled out my noodle

And boingy bouncy too.

I'm flip flap happy.

I'm as giddy as a jig.

Like a dog in a butcher's excited

Or in a mud bath, like a pig.

I'm wavy, jumpy, jiving.

I'm sane. I've not gone mad.

I wake up every morning,

Thinking the best news I've had.

I'm flam flum flying.

I'm seeing with new eyes.

I understood that God is real,

Despite the tuts and sighs.

No lies or delusion.

No hamster wheel confusion.

No nefarious plot to control you

With your-downfall-in-mind collusion,

With the state,

illuminati or invisible elite…

This is free. It's grace.

From a saviour you can meet.

Who walked in the dust;
in the mire;
In the grime.
Who died for me and you.
Incredible. Divine.

MYSELF (A NOD TO 'ME' BY R. MCGOUGH)

If I were big
I'd want to be a mouse

If I were little
I'd want to be a house

If I were a muffin
I'd want to be cake

If I were ice- cream
I'd want to be steak

If I were a drink
I'd want to be food

If I were a circus act
I'd want to be a snood

If I were a fairground stall
I'd want to be a car

If I were a hermit
I'd want to be a star

If I were a tree
I'd want to be a sweet

If I were a car
I'd want to be a sheet

If I were a mountain
I'd want to be sea

If I could be anyone else
I'd be as happy as could be.

DO YOU?

Do you remember when God refused to mention you, his adored child, on any posts on social media?

Do you remember when God was too busy for you during the week, apart from once on a Sunday when he was distracted and not really listening to you?

Do you remember when you gave him so many wonderful gifts but he couldn't do the same for you?

Do you remember when he refused to even mention you to friends or family because he felt awkward or worried about what they'd say?

Do you remember how he would ignore you, refuse to listen to your wishes and rarely ever listen to your advice?

Do you remember him saying he must be part of your family because he 'occasionally speaks to you?'

Do you remember all the times everything was more of a priority to him, than you?

Do you remember him telling a couple of people he was your dad but then having nothing to do with you?

Do you remember him doing any of this?!!!

Me neither.

JUST ASK...

Asking for help
Isn't weak, giving up
Or cowardice.
It takes courage.
Sometimes,
The bravest thing
You can ever say is
'Please can you help me?!'

GOD IS... A-Z

Dear God, I just want to thank you for (being):

A: Amazing, awesome, accepting, always-near, Abba, artist, artistic-director, author, answer, almighty, able, Alpha, answers,

B: Brilliant, bodacious, balm, barrier, blesses, bold, beautiful

C: Calm, cares, creative, calling, calls, community, communication, choreographer, chooses, comforter, closest-friend, cardiologist, constant, consistent, celebration, counsellor, compassionate, creator, companion, centre, calls us,

D: Driven, dedicated, divine, doting, destiny, director, dance, destined, discerning, Dad, draws, dancing,

E: Endless, exciting, enveloping, everywhere, (is) everything, enjoyment, expects, exceptional, endures, equality, eye-opening, enlivening, eternal, enables

F: Friend, father, fearless, forgiving, flawless, for-us, freedom, fun, funny, faith, faithful, first, fair, fierce, flamboyant,

G: Generous, Glorious, giving, great, gregarious, governs, gigantic, grace, graceful, glorified, gardener, guides, good, governs, gives,

H: Holy, heavenly, heart, hope, healer, heals, helper, hears, healing,

I: Incredible, inside-us, important, intuitive, incomprehensible, incomparable, inventor, inventive, intelligent, intolerant-to-sin, interested in us, inspiring, Immanuel,

J: Just, jealous, joy, judge, Jehovah, jubilation

K: Kindness, key-to-life, knows-best, key, King, knows-us-best, King of kings, knocks

L: Love, life, laughter, Lord, light, listening, language, listens,

M: Mighty, marvellous, most-high, music, merciful, miraculous, meaning, majesty

N: New-every-morning, noble, never ending, nurturing, needed, near, nissi, nudges,

O: Omnipresent, omniscient, omnipotent, open, overall, Omega,

P: Perfect, peace, present, papa, persistent, plans, planned, poet, potter, protects, provider, perfect, patient, purpose,

Q: Quiet, quintessential, quirky,

R: Redeemer, royal, right, righteous, roar, respectful, restoration, restorer, real, relevant, righteous, right, rock, relationship, remover, reliable, robust, refuge,

S: Saves-us, saviour, sanctuary, sanctification, still, strength, solid, solidarity, Spirit, strong, sculptor, song, speaks to us, salt, stronghold, softens, sure, stunning, sacrifices, specific, strong, steadfast, steady, surprising,

T: Truth, trustworthy, tremendous, treasure, true, there, talks to us, tower, trinity, truth, teacher, transformation,

U: Understanding, unity, universal, unimaginable, unstoppable, unique, upright, utilises, unexpected,

V: Voice, variety, value, venerable, vibrant,

W: Wholeness, wind, whisper, working, wise, Wisdom, wow, warrior, wild, wrath, wonderful

X: xenophile, Xenophon,

Y: Yahweh, Yes, yearns,

Z: zealous

I really don't have the words to say how grateful I am to you so please give me your strength, to offer every part of my life as a 'thank offering' to you.

Calum

A NEGATIVE PREGNANCY TEST

Today we learned that
You weren't really there -
Beautiful beautiful one.
Today all our nerves
Fluttered away like moths
Beautiful beautiful one.

Today all our plans,
Milestones and tears, drifted off
Beautiful beautiful one.
Today your siblings' hopes
Of a new friend, vanished
Beautiful beautiful one.

You were never there;
Your mum was never pregnant
You were talked and laughed about.
You were imagined in vivid technicolour.
You would have been another miracle.

Our beautiful, beautiful one.

HELD (FOR MY WIFE, WHO IS WELSH, LAURA)

Come and rest in my arms
My love.
In roots and bracken and flowers,
With nests and heather in my hair;
With wild honey on my lips;
With thorns and nettles that may scratch,
I will hold you.
I will love you.
Though our journey may be drenched in
Angry, storm-roared rain,
Though you may be tempted to doubt
My love,
I promise that if you will only come to
My arms,
I will hold you until your turbulent soul finds
Peace.

APRIL PRAYER 2

Dear God,

Please help me to keep going on days when I feel you're far away.

Please give me the strength to have faith and to 'hide your words in my heart so I might not sin against you'.

May you show me if there is any sin I need to confess.

Please help me understand more of your grace and who you are.

Thank you for your patience and unfailing love.

Calum

I SCREAM

If I was an ice cream

I think I'd be vanilla

With dark, bitter

Chocolate chips,

Popping candy

With illuminous pink

Swirls of

strawberry

Sauce...

LEARNING TO WALK (FIRST WEEKS AS A CHRISTIAN)

I stumble and fall, several times a day.

Sometimes I mix it up and

Take three steps back,

Fall down, feel sorry for myself

Then take a step forward,

Before tripping over my own feet...

I listen to the lies that tell me

It's not worth it.

I'm a failure.

What's the point?

I'm finding it harder, not easier...

And the classic -

'Everyone else has got it together;

What's wrong with you?!'

I want to be like you.

I want to tell people good news.

I want this damaged, paranoid, defensive,

Scrappy, impatient and melancholy heart,

To be replaced with yours.

I want to love others before myself and

Not react to the slightest thing.

I want to see people through your eyes.

I want to forgive, even if it hurts…

I just find it so hard.

UNIMAGINABLE

A rhapsody in blue

And every hue,

From yellow to green.

Trying to imagine colours

You and I have never seen.

Symphonic delight,

in every shade of green;

Try and think of a colour

That's never been.

BABEL

Poems build inside me;

A thousand voices

Who refuse to speak

In one consistent tongue

Or form…

Scaling layer upon layer,

Whispering, reverberating echoes

Of those I admire:

Keats, Zephaniah, Milligan, Cope, Rosen,

Angelou, Sissay, Stevie Smith, Auden.

Then mixing with the multitude of

Garbled cacophony in my head.

Climbing higher.

Building.

Until they reach the freedom of

my mouth or pen,

Hoping that, in being released to the world,

They will find a language of their own.

WHERE AM I FROM?

When people ask me where I'm from, I can answer simply regarding my place of birth or I can explain my parents' Scottish and English heritage...

I'm from the Scottish highlands - beautiful and harsh countryside; People with inner steel, grit and salt spray in their beards. I'm also from Romany Gypsies who's roots shifted with their families - oppressed for thousands of years.

I'm from the rolling, bleak, astounding dales of Yorkshire, England, where folk are friendly and a cup of tea or a pint solves most ailments; Tough, weathered and jaw-dropping.

I'm from the traditions of story tellers that can be traced back to the dawn of time; tales of the hunt, told by the fire; bellies sated. I'm from the Greek theatre actors, philosophical orators and poets of China, India and French troubadours.

I'm from Elizabethan theatre, Shakespeare, Wordsworth, Rossetti, Kipling, Owen, Heaney, McGough, Rosen......I'm from Reggae and Rap.....eighties and nineties....Tupac to Eminem to Dave the Poet....

I'm from Rogers & Hammerstein, Larsson, Sondheim and Lloyd-Weber. I'm from speeches by Bilocca, Pankhurst and Wilberforce using words to create change.

I'm from Larkin, Armitage, Cope, Zephaniah, Angelou and Sissay. I'm from Tik-Tok, YouTube and Instagram writers - demanding to be heard in new ways. I'm from slam poetry, rap battles and people sharpening each others' skills.

I'm from Connolly to Robin Williams to Kevin Bridges...I'm from all the authors who inspired my imagination - setting off a chain of explosives that made words become living things - Steinbeck to Coelho to Huxley to C.S Lewis....

I'm from Psalms to Proverbs to The Song of Solomon. I'm from parables revealing beautiful truths. I'm from the Gospels to letters to prophecies...

I come from written, spoken, shared and offered words of hope and love and joy that have seeped into my bones, in ways that no one in my family tree ever could.

These are my roots and these are where I'm from...

But if you want the easy answer......I'm from Lincoln.

OUTSIDE THE CITY WALLS...

A leper, excited by having been healed, returned to the gates of Jerusalem's

'outcast colony';

'Come and meet a man who healed me.

He's the son of God.'

His friends came to the gate and sneered:

'Who does he think he is?!'

Other friends were kinder and less bothered:

'He can believe what he wants.

If it makes him happy so what?

I don't believe him though.'

The man came back, day after day...

'I've been healed and I'm free.

There's a whole world out here that you're

Missing out on. Come and meet him.'

By now a crowd had gathered at the gate:

'You're insulting our rights. We don't care.

You're a pawn. Maybe you healed yourself'.

The man, even from a distance saw

The scars, wounds and prison

His friends were enduring...

Even when he explained about Jesus

And the healing he'd received;

They mocked, were uninterested and

Refused to see their own need or the one who could make them whole.

MY WIFE WON'T BELIEVE ME...

She says she's not a poet,

Which is, in part, why I know she is…

With no airs or graces,

She writes lines and affirmations

In the notes on her phone

And the hearts of our kids.

Belief in them, playing with them,

Being patient long after my patience ends.

Her grandad wrote poetry

So I know it's part of her soul and genes.

She writes feelings and takes time

To consider each and every individual

line and phrase,

Unlike my rushed, frantic grappling

With poems like holding on to

A tiger's tale.

She's my champion, my hero, the reason I

Started to write again and if a poet or poem

Has a human form, It's her.

WARM GLOW ON A COLD DAY

I realised one day 'I want to live…'

It might not sound much but it had crept up on me.

I'd become a Christian

A few days before.

I sat there on a grey, drizzly day

Basking in the warm, rays of hope.

'I want to live…'

'I want to live…'

Saying it tasted like eating

Fresh raspberries or strawberries & cream.

'I want to live…'

So I'm going to do so for God.

A WARNING ABOUT STORIES

Tell stories of all kinds to your children;

But be careful and aware

Of what stories

You tell

Yourself.

APRIL PRAYER

Dear God,

Please bring peace to our house and let it be used to bring glory to you.

May your calm and Holy Spirit fill it and may we have the words to tell our kids about you.

Please give us the strength to love, forgive and serve each other as you have done for us.

Please let any visitors or delivery people feel your presence.

May you use this place for any purpose you see fit and please help us to be patient with our kids.

Thank you for this house and garden. Thank you for your providence and generosity.

In Jesus' name.

Calum

Q AND M BANQUET MENU:

(Exodus chapter 16)

- Quail stew
- Roasted Quail
- Quail wrap
- Boiled quail
- Stir fried quail
- Quail paratha
- Quail soup
- Quail on slices of baked Manna
- Quail sandwich
- Poached quail
- Quail and Manna dumplings
- Barbecued quail
- Steamed quail
- Quail surprise
- Quail of the day.
- Manna pretzels.
- Manna flatbreads.
- Manna dumplings filled with quail
- Manna loaf cooked on hot-coals

This is a fixed menu for the next 40 years. Please remember to throw away any left over Manna at the end of each day or you will wake up to it covered in worms and stinking like an Egyptian's latrine.

God will provide daily Manna, except on Fridays when you will be provided with double so you don't have to collect any on the sabbath.

TWO QUOTES:

('You are a slave to whatever you desire'
and
'There is no such thing as true freedom!')

What do we want?

Freedom.

When do we want it?

Now!

What if you never can?

Now!

What if you'll always be enslaved by something?

Now!

What if even the rich, famous or hippies aren't free?

Now!!!

What do you want?

We want freedom.

When do you want it?

Now!

MY LIFEGUARD

My lifeguard walks on water;

He calms the stormy waves.

If you're floundering

Or feel like you're drowning,

Be certain, Jesus saves.

IN NEED OF HEART SURGERY

Why doesn't my heart break for those who aren't saved, the way it does when my kids are in pain?

Why don't I bow down in prayer as much as my head bows down to look at my phone?

Why don't I get as excited about heaven as I do about time with my family?

Why do I find it easier to judge others than think about what they're dealing with?

Why does telling you 'I love you' feel so strange on my lips but saying it to my kids comes naturally?

YOU'VE GOT THIS

I've been praying and praying;

As storms began to roll in with

Rumbled thunder and

Clawed-hand lightning.

In the past few weeks

I've been struggling because

Sometimes you *seem* so distant; So quiet.

At other times I *feel* like my prayers

Are being called out in a cave;

Bouncing back to me as echoes…

I just wanted to write this though Lord

Because I know, beyond know, beyond know

That you are working.

Even when I can't see it.

Even when I doubt you.

Even when I feel far away.

You're answering prayer.

You're teaching me.

You're in control.

INDEPENDENCE

My idealised, angelic youngest

Is becoming difficult;

Her attitude, lack of manners and

Deceitful ness are sneaking through

Cracks in her previously-pristine

Porcelain veneer.

She's tougher.

More opinionated.

She answers back; which is new.

She is starting to stamp or rebel

Or bite back;

I am torn between *relief*

and *mourning*

Who she once was.

BECAUSE OF JESUS, THIS IS WHO YOU ARE...

(Based on a Craig Roeschel sermon)

In a dark world,

You're the light that shines.

When you walk into a room,

Light walks into a room;

Hope walks into a room;

Faith walks into a room.

By the words of the testimony

Of what Jesus did for you.

By the death and blood

Of Jesus, you are an overcomer.

You are not who others say you are.

How they react doesn't determine

Your worth.

You're who God says you are

And he says you're chosen;

He says you're loved.

He says you have a purpose.

In Christ. You are an overcomer.

THE BEST (OR WORST) IS YET TO COME.

If you have chosen

To follow Jesus,

This is as close

To hell that you will ever be.

The best is yet to come.

If you have chosen

To ignore Jesus,

This is as close

To heaven you will ever be.

The worst is yet to come.

PINE TREE

I will go there to sit a while

And mourn all that is lost.

I will grieve for myself,

My grandparents and

All those missed opportunities.

I will etch names of past loves

Into the trunk so deeply,

My great-grandchildren

Will wonder who took

Residence in my soul

And never

Left.

MISTAKE

Is still

Bloody.

Please take

It back.

I want

It black.

ANOTHER SCHOOL SHOOTING

How many children

Needed to be

Killed in schools

Before senators and

Some Americans see

That some things

Are more important

Than their outdated,

Constitutional

'Rights'?!

LIES

The world would be better without you in it.

You are trapped.

The world would be better without you in it.

You have no choices.

The world would be better without you in it.

You don't have anyone who will listen.

The world would be better without you in it.

You are worthless and a waste of air.

The world would be better without you in it.

You shouldn't speak to a doctor.

The world would be better without you in it.

You have no one in your life who cares.

The world would be better without you in it.

You will always be stuck and things won't get better.

The world would be better without you in it.

You should know this is THE ONLY answer.

The world would be better without you in it.

Lies, lies, lies, lies, lies, lies,lies and lies.

If we can see them for what they are, maybe we can start to see…..*the truth.*

FICKLE

He loves you until you're out of sight,

Like the rising sun forgets night.

RIGHT. NOW.

God is answering prayer.

Things are moving into place.

Realisations are being had.

Hearts are being softened.

People are finding out prayers have been answered.

God is manoeuvring things into place.

Things are dissolving or growing.

God is listening.

God is ready to answer your heart's cry, if you'll just call out to him.

Right. Now.

CHEESE PLAYLIST:

Lady in Red Leicester

Sweet dreams are made of cheese.

Relax! (Fondue it)

Don't stop Brie-lieving.

Nobody does it feta.

Let it Brie.

Swiss me.

I gotta Gouda feelin.

Roule the world.

Edam I wish I was your lover.

Jailhouse Roquefort

If you (Dairy)lea-ve me now.

Quarklife!

THE NEED TO CREATE

I want to create splatter art

And write for days

I want to dance on a beach

And sing in strange ways.

I want to sculpt with clay

And write a screenplay.

I want to take photographs

And create all day.

I want to make art from nature

And perform on stage.

I want to design things I build

And paint in all colours but beige.

I want to build with odd materials

And write a novel or two.

I want to direct theatre

And salsa dance, when blue.

I want to play instruments

And play in a band.

I want karaoke nights

And build sculptures in the sand.

I want to tattoo art work

And create new shades of red.

I want to create

For the Lord who died in my stead.

MARCH PRAYER 3

Dear God,

Thank you for all the good and great things in the world:

For kindness shown to others. For all the varied and beautiful colours of nature. For laughter. For music. For love. For generosity.

For all the wonderful and strange creatures on land, in the air and in the sea.

For the uplifting gift of friendship. For families. For all the different types of food and the love that is put into making it. For achievement. For new life. For the wisdom and experience of age.

For the strength to face life's trials. For the arts. For helping people realise their potential. For sunsets and sunrises. For answered prayer. For the acceptance you and loved ones give us.

For all the variety of humans with their gifts, languages and personalities.

Thank you that so much of what you have created is for our, and your, enjoyment.

Thank you for giving your son to die in our place and for your forgiveness.

Calum

ONE DAY WE'RE ACTUALLY GOING TO BE IN HEAVEN!

Take all the best bits of life:

Love, cake, family holidays, tax rebates, smashing a job interview, sunsets, sunrises, sex, hearing 'I love you', saying 'I love you', water slides, sweets, holding your child for the first time, Christmas morning, your kids' laughter, eating with friends and family, flowers...

...the sea, donuts, giving gifts that make people smile, helping people, singing, dancing, writing, reading, being on a train, fireworks, Chinese food, chocolate, learning something new, farting, compliments...

...visiting new countries, rollercoasters, rain, playing in snow, Indian food, snorkelling, photography, chippy teas, hugs, Christmas

Eve, Easter, volunteering, new foods, laughing so hard you cry, looking at someone you love across a crowded room (knowing what each other is thinking), music, lie ins; crisp, clean bedding; fresh coffee; seeing your children achieve what they previously believed they couldn't do,

Hide & seek, board games (but not Monopoly)

Reconnecting with old friends, camping, swimming in a cold lake on a warm day, smiles; a blanket, book, warm drink and a cat on your lap, on a cold day; Autumn's colours...

Then combine the happiness in them all, multiply it by a million and *still* it's nowhere near how happy we will be (and how wonderful it will be) when we get to heaven and be with our father and maker.

IF YOUR...

If your brain works in wiggly lines, out the box;

if you're comfortable wearing bright un-matched socks;

If you have to get up and dance when the song plays;

If you like playing at the park on swings for days,

We're destined to be mates.

If you dance around your kitchen with absolute glee,

If you need to feel you own a choice, to feel free,

If you have a thirst to read and learn each day;

If you're a person who does things their own way,

It's true, we should be friends.

If you believe manners and punctuality are gold,

If you feel like the kid who never grew old,

If you'd rather buy bargains and second- hand clothes,

If you're addicted to reading both poetry and prose,

We should definitely be pals.

If you're loyal and empathetic when your friends are down,

If you're ambivert inclined and need a room with no sound,

If you feel creative things all the time;

If your senses are tickled by art or a rhyme,

We should most definitely be friends.

A CAST OF POETIC PLAYERS

A hyperbole dances on the screen

While the similes and metaphors preen;

Alliteration sits silently seething-

Personification, loudly breathing.

A formidable syllable stamps in time,

Soon joined by the siblings 'rhythm and rhyme'.

Repetition tap, tap, tap,taps on the stage

Contrast whispers with a screaming rage.

Onomatopoeia makes a bang, crash, croak

Meaning's sat hiding under a black cloak.

When the cast have gathered on my imaginary stage,

I pick up my pen and start to write on the page.

MUFFLED CHRISTMAS

(letter from an absent Dad)

Sweetheart

On this Silent Night,

Know

That I might not be there

To kiss your head

And wish you

Festive joy

But my wee boy,

You are on my mind.

In this Christmas spell,

Where company

Determines heaven

From Purgatory or Hell,

Know full well

You are the greatest

Present and the best of my

past and future.

My joy to the world,

My far off star,

Sleep contently far from sight,

On this Christmas, Silent Night.

(written the first Christmas away from my eldest child, after my first marriage ended in 2008)

I HAVEN'T LOST MY MIND...A TESTIMONY IN RHYME

I'm not mad or medically insane.

I've had no damage to any part

Of my brain.

I've not been hypnotised

Or been fooled to give money.

I've not joined a cult

Where people talk funny.

I've not reached rock bottom

With no joy or choices.

I don't see hallucinations

Or hear voices.

I had no desire to search for a God

Who I mocked and called names like

'Uncaring' or 'odd'.

I had no addictions.

I committed no crime.

I didn't lose everything

Then asked for a sign.

I quite simply wanted

To see what evidence was there.

I didn't expect much
Or really care.
I read and I questioned
And to my surprise,
My Heavenly Father
Opened my eyes;
I felt real peace
That wasn't in my head,
That followed just after a prayer
I'd said.
He's changed my life
And I talk to him
Each day.
I want to live for God as
He is The Way.

SURROUNDED

There's wonderful, incredible, omnipresent

And divine

Stories all around us

All of the time;

In the lines of a rust-red leaf

To a spider's artistic web.

In the veins on bark

To the waves that ebb.

In the buzzing of a bee

Or the layers of a rose

We're surrounded constantly

By poetry and prose.

SURROUNDED IN WINTER

There's wonderful, incredible, omnipresent

And divine

Stories all around us

All of the time;

In the lines of an icy leaf

To a spider's frozen, artistic web.

In the veins on pine bark

To the waves that sigh and ebb.

In the smoking, warming chimneys

Or the calming softness of snows

We're surrounded constantly

By poetry and prose.

MY FIRST MARRIAGE

You left

And

I finally

Breathed

WRAPPED IN A BOW

I asked for abstract nouns

For Christmas

And for them to be wrapped with a bow.

Peace, love, hope, happiness,

Bag em up

Wrap em up.

Ho Ho Ho.

NEVER FORGET....

Never forget:

To let us know you're safe

To keep yourself safe

To look both ways.

Never forget

To tell the truth or

To expect the truth.

To check your change.

Never forget

To do your best.

To not fret, if you've done your best.

To check the doors at night.

Never forget:

To trust God has a plan (and purpose)

For your life, if you'll just trust him.

To refuse to give up on your dreams

To make sure you have big dreams

To be careful who you trust.

Never forget God loves you

And cares about you.

Never forget we love you

In more ways than we can explain.

Never forget

We are always here.

Love Mum & Dad x

TENACITY

Those who do the things

that most won't,

get the results

that most don't!

THE CON

You punched out
My heart, my hope,
My senses,
While everyone else
Watched through
Rose coloured
Lenses.

MADE WHOLE BY GOLD

Sharon Malone

Was cracked and broken

By the fists of others;

And by words spoken.

She couldn't recognise herself

When she observed her reflection..

Cracked and distorted was her comprehension .

Eventually the healing started to pour,

Like molten gold, it left her feeling raw.

She never saw herself as she used to be

But something newer, she wore beautifully.

God had made her stronger;

A sight to behold.

Her cracks and flaws

Were now filled with his gold.

MY TODDLER YEARS IN A HOUSE OF DOMESTIC ABUSE

I was born to a world of

Shifting tectonic plates

Where every morning,

Volcanoes would erupt

And the fog of the first

Ten cigarettes

Preceded daily battle ground

Cries, among the ruins of

Our drifting life.

As plates smashed and fell

Among my he-man figures

And Millennium Falcon,

Blows were traded

(As old bruises faded)

With violence constantly

In my emerging peripheral vision…

A dad was *someone who smashed the house up,*

A mother was *someone who screamed and hit dad.*

I've been told my temper raged like a mini-tornado,

As I screamed obscenities that I'd learned by rote.

Each morning, I'd wait to see which parents (or mood)would be lurking in the lounge, like an under fed troll; *hangry.*

Lego creations were often smashed by me

Because *'that's what grown-ups do.'*

I spent hours crying to myself and listening at doors for the merest hint of eruption…

…as an adult those fears linger but have transformed into mental health diagnosis

And psychosis…..

On quiet mornings I still fear the rage and destruction outside…

And within.

POOR PHILOSOPHY

It's November now;

Shall we eat

Or heat?

PHOTOGRAPHS

I tore you out the photographs

And tidied some out the way.

I wish I could do the same with my heart,

As I miss you

Every day.

MARCH PRAYER 2

Dear God,

I don't know why you don't answer prayer sometimes. It's a bit disheartening but I understand I'm a young Christian.

Please help me trust you.

Please either answer my prayer or give me the strength and patience, while you teach me what I need to learn.

I know I'm new to this Christian thing and I am so grateful for all you've done for me. I'm sorry that I doubt you sometimes or get impatient or worried.

Please teach me and help me.

Calum

TIME-TRAVELLER

I exist

in

Yesterday's

Tomorrow

And

Tomorrow's

Yesterday.

The past

And

Present,

Breathe

In this

Moment.

SIGHTS AND SOUNDS I HOPE MY KIDS REMEMBER

I find myself struggling to remember large gigabytes of memory of my childhood,

While the megabytes I do find are spoiled or painful.

When I look at my kids I hope that their childhood memories are:

The smell of Sunday roasts, fire-pits, roasted marshmallows and the sea.

The taste of Christmas dinner, soups in winter and sweets they bought with their own money.

The sight of eating together as a family every day, me and my wife dancing together or the magic of the first snowfall or frost.

The sounds of laughter, every kind of music played in the kitchen or the words 'I love you'…

…The feeling of being hugged daily, having their heads stroked when ill; or the crinkly, shining paper, unwrapped at Christmas.

That these will be what they remember and that the other parts will, hopefully, melt away.

SCENTS OF TIME

Mornings carry scents of fresh, damp Hope…dew on flowers…unspoiled smells of grass, moss and steaming coffee.

Mid-day carries the aroma of dry, dehydrated sun rays…fire-cracker bangs of conversations, while lunches, washed-cars and conkers grapple to be imbued.

Early evenings smell heavier…rich, earthy and slightly bitter…exhausts of growling roads…drizzle, noise and leaf-mulch…wood smoke and roast dinners zapping the air.

Midnight is rich like coffee or liquorice…the smells of rest; clean and empty…passing wisps of alcohol soaked home-wanderers; embers trickling from shivering chimneys…a dark, clean, slate; it's the scent of 'nothing more can be done today.'

HOW DO YOU GRIEVE THE LIVING DEAD?

How do you grieve the living dead?...

The friends who ghosted you or stopped trying...

The family member who battles addiction or

The person who changed so much,

You have to put distance between you,

For your sake?

There's no cards, flowers or lines of people

Offering (real or fake)sympathy.

There's no 'wake' celebrating the good and daft and
bittersweet!

No one texts to see how you're holding up or brings a meal
over because you're 'grief tired'.

There's no end.

Just a pulsing, pressing,

claustrophobic, awareness that they're gone..

And yet...not.

That the person they were (or what you had) isn't there
anymore...

They aren't buried, burned, dropped in the ocean; they still exist…

A wound that never fully heals.

A scab that's often picked.

A death that isn't death.

A used to be.

A ghost.

Where are the eulogies and hugs and being able to cry, then heal…

For that?

GOD IS A:

Joy giver

Light bringer

Strong tower

Refreshing spring

Immovable mountain

Firm foundation

Soul soother

Master potter

Protective shield

Glorious sun

Perfect father

Extravagant artist

Just judge

Patient teacher

Closest companion

Roaring lion

Calm oasis

Resolute truth

Life's fountain

Caring shepherd

My God,

My Abba,

My soul's rest

My creator.

My Dad.

SOOTHED

Noise on window panes.

Dark skies.

Empty streets;

Forcing the village into

A lockdown,

That soothes my

Parched

Soul.

PEACHES

My tongue dances and tickles the soft stubble,

Before fragile skin tears,

Releasing soft, sweet, satisfying juice

Down my chin;

Which I slurp hungrily.

This peach has been sitting

In my fridge all day,

Just so I can experience cooling syrup

On my burning face.

I tear off pieces of felt-like skin

Delicately dangling them above my mouth

Before letting them dissolve

on my parched tongue.

As I eat through the ice-cold, syrupy, flesh

I reach the stone and pick it out

(With stubby, nail-bitten fingers)

Throwing it through the window

Onto the soil outside…

Optimistic that a tree will grow someday.

I keep the remaining half for desert;

When I will sprinkle sugar on it,

Place it under the grill, then adorn with

Finely chopped red chillies, lime juice

And rich vanilla ice cream,

Like a rich crown on a sweet Queen.

PLEASE CHANGE ME TO BE MORE LIKE YOU

Please don't leave me as I am Lord.

I don't want to stay this way.

I want to become more like you;

At least a bit, every day.

Please don't let me stay the same Lord.

I don't want to be the 'old me'.

I want to feel your love for others.

I want to walk, knowing I'm free.

Please keep moulding me Lord.

I want to be shaped to your will.

I want to show fruits of your Spirit.

I want my anxious mind to be still.

Please make me more like you Lord.

I want to learn more each day.

I want to know what you want me to do.

I don't want to be the same way.

THE LIGHTHOUSE KEEPER

A lighthouse keeper, long ago grew tired
In his role…he had been so excited as a
Young man, given the keys to this beacon
Of light; it felt important. It was important.
He would see boats, large and small
Avoiding rocks and other dangers
Because he made sure he shone his light.
People would gratefully blast their horns.
That was a long time ago.
Recently people had begun to ignore him,
Waving banners declaring 'we'll decide'.
He'd run downstairs, standing on the rocks
Shouting and waving…
They shouted or shone morse code signals
'You can't tell us what to do!'
'We can decide our own way.'
'You're offending other ways we could go.'
He saw many accidents, injuries and lost
Travellers - some of whom drifted until they
Starved, despite avoiding crashing.
Why couldn't they just follow the light?

Each night, he checks, fixes and cleans
To make sure his light is bright and seen.
Despite the ones who ignored him,
It always made him smile each time
Someone sailed to safety.
He would keep doing his job,
Until the chief Lighthouse Commander
Informed him that he was ready to go home.

GOD'S HEART

Every time you cried,

It broke my heart.

Every wound you suffered

Did not go unnoticed.

I looked on,

Hoping you would turn to me.

See, I made you with a unique,

Specific blend of abilities, personality traits

And things you care about deeply,

To fulfil your purpose, that I made you for.

In fact, I sacrificed my own son.

Every time you cried, I was there.

Every time you angrily shouted I wasn't real,

I was there.

Every time you were scared, I was there…

Waiting for you to turn to me.

I love you. I will never leave you.

I want you to see that you need forgiveness

Through my son, who came back to life

Three days later so I can make you whole.

I love you and I promise you

I bring life in it's fullness.

I've heard your cries.

I've seen your wounds and scars.

If you'll recognise your need for me

And live the way I want you to live,

Then I promise you, your life can truly…

Begin.

WHERE THE SUN SETS

Standing at the edge

Of an endless sea

Where I can't see you

On the horizon and

Where every wave

takes my legs from under

Me....

A place where,

Just as I think

I can stand again,

Another wave steals

My ability to stand-

Rolling over me,

Seeking to drown me,

While I still look for you

Where the sun sets.

WINK

I looked over at her,

From across the car park

And caught her eye…

I took it back to her

And smiled.

It was love

At first sight.

FOREST

Sun lasers through gaps in trees

And refracts into rainbows

Through rain soaked leaves

While I take big, relieving,

Sustenance-bringing air, into my lungs….

And cry.

<u>JOY</u>

The first time
I held yours
And my kids'
Hands;

The first time
You called me 'husband'
And they called me 'Dad'.

GROWTH

We often don't see that we are growing

Until we start bearing fruit.

Most of the time we're weathering storms,

Waiting, getting stronger and taking in essential nutrients....

Trust God.

You're growing.

Even when it's imperceptible.

MY ELDEST CHILD NEARS BEING SIXTEEN

He sits with a permanent scowl;
Like he's learned to protect himself
With a refusal to smile at things
That previously brought him joy.
My wee boy slopes and slumps off,
Encased in the body of a man
He's not grown into yet.
The sparkle doesn't reach his eyes
When he laughs anymore.
His mumbles and grunts display
Some sort of reverse evolution.
I lament and grieve being able
To pick him up so I can tickle and
Hug him back to being happy.
I mourn for the person who I
No longer know.
Despite being a teenager once,
I feel he's growing out of reach;
Far from my care, my nurture and my love.

DIGNITY

He leans
Ever so slightly
On his mahogany cane;
Pink carnations
Nestled safely
In the crook
Of his arm.
His left arm
Moves slowly to
Touch his cap
And tap it gently,
as he
Greets everyone
With a 'good morning'
Controlling the tears,
Like a backed up damn,
To, and from,
Where his true love
Lays buried.

MARCH PRAYER

Dear God,

I've been praying and I'm grateful for the requests you've answered. Truly.

I've enjoyed the silent prayer times. The worship prayer times; and the washing up times.

I'm a bit stuck on the 'prayer request' times though…I don't get it! If your will is perfect and you know what we need before we say something, then why ask you? Also, sometimes you say no so how do we know if we're asking for the right thing? Why do you need our faith?

I know beyond know beyond know, you're all powerful but I just don't get it.

Please help me understand,

Calum

AUTUMN HAIKU

Leaves curl, changing colour

Rain pours while fallen leaves mulch

Bare trees bow in praise.

SHADOW

For so long

I've been scared of you

But now I realise

That the huge, menacing, imposing, looming, suffocating

Figure I thought you were,

Was only a shadow,

Cast by a small man,

On the wall of the cave

You tried to keep me in.

SWEATY

We walked down the road,

Our hands occasionally grazing each other,

With a spark and a crackle

As we briefly connected.

Your hands were wet with sweat

So when I finally took your hand

For the first time,

The electricity was conducted

By the water

And the pulsing thrum of desire,

Need and connection.

Twelve years later

And that crackle of want and need

Still passes through us in electric charge,

When we walk down the road

And I take your, still nervous,

Sweaty hand in mine.

PAVLOV'S PEOPLE

Semi-educated people

Like to patronisingly laugh

At Pavlov's stupid dogs

Without realising

That we are just like those canines…

As our phones buzz or ring

With another

Notification and

gratification.

WILD

I have a wild garden,

With stubborn grass and flowers

pushing between the stones;

Demanding to grow and be seen.

Where the orange poppies

Reach for the sun in constant longing.

I have a wild garden

With hundreds of unspent wishes,

Sitting atop of dandelions

And where laughter-drops fall between

The paving stones,

soaking the ground below.

I have a wild garden

With football goals chalked on the walls,

Decorated with marauding

flowers and vines…

While roses and blackberries

Dance and wrestle by the big gates.

I have a wild garden

That is in love with water;

Splashes from the paddling pool,

Spray from the hosepipe amidst giggles

From running children and

From thirst-quenching, lashing rain.

I have a wild garden

That reminds me growth and aspirations

Win through;

That sunlight, water and goodness

swell hearts and spark growth...

That shedding or pruning leads to abundance.

The stones, plants and grass are soaked in

Laughter, love and smiles because...

I have a wild garden.

PRODUCT RE-CALL

2022-05 Recall: United Kingdom r.e Conservative Government

The following notice has been issued by the 'Standards for living' agency (SLA) regarding the United Kingdom's government.

Product details:

A Conservative government that have repeatedly made cuts to the most vulnerable in society, broken promises, arrogantly broken rules THEY made and shown not the merest hint of compassion, led by a leader who has the moral compass of a medieval ruler.

Best before date: as soon as possible

Risk statement:

Debt, further mental ill health, lack of nutrition/calories, reliance on food banks, societal division, actions that are made with impunity, pensions being taken…ad infinitum

Action taken by the company:

A small percentage are voting for change but many seem 'Boris Blind' unable to see the wrong being done to them or others…ideally the company (sic 'The United Kingdom) should recall the product and cease to continue or relaunch in future.

Our advice to customers:

Write to M.Ps. Protest. Organise and protest. Open your eyes. Do not cast votes or invest in this product in the future.

Warning:

Failure to ignore our advice will put you and those you love, at risk of further mistreatment and hardship.

CELSIUS

Heat waves

But cold

Bites

I REALLY DON'T KNOW...

Half stooped,

She pulls the microphone towards her

As though cradling an ice-cream

On a blistering Summer's day.

Smoke hangs in the air,

Distorting faces-

While a sea of headless bodies pause.....

Still.

With each line and note

The heartbreak and loss

Balances on a tightrope of memories

Too painful to recall.

Whiskey numbed vocal chords

Speak of raw, broken hearts

And whispered, deafening rage.

Polite patrons politely clap and praise,

Which soothes her lonely soul,

As her song closes....

.....' I really don't know life....at all.'

GOOSEBUMPS

If a goose holds wings with another goose

For the first time,

If they see their breathtaking, heart-stopping goose-wife
walking down the aisle,

If their child nearly gets hurt but narrowly

escapes,

If they accidentally touch a slug or snail,

Or if they hear a beautiful goosey aria or perfect harmony,

Or randomly feel shivery as though

some-goose has walked over their grave.....

Do they just feel 'bumps'?

TELL YOUR STORY; IT'S YOUR DUTY

Film it,

Write a poem,

Draw a picture,

Paint the abstract,

Start a podcast,

Do a blog…or vlog,

Write a play.

Tik-Tok,

Write a novel.

Start a band.

Write a song,

Act.

Sing.

Start a YouTube channel.

Write a memoir.

Create a sculpture.

Take photographs…

Set-design sets,

Direct,

Write a screenplay…

Please.

Just.

Tell.

Your.

Story.

Someone

Needs

To

Hear

It.

MY BRITISH BLENDED FAMILY

My Mum's from Yorkshire,

Dad's from Inverness;

I've got Northern Grit

But got married in a dress.

I like to eat haggis

Or me Yorkshire pud

I've got my dad's ears

But me mam's iron blood

Raised in Scotland

Raised in't Dales

Married a woman - slate strong,

From Wales

Our welsh cakes sit with oat cakes

As we sip Yorkshire tea,

There in't owt else but British

About ma wee family.

UNNERVED

My black cat left a dismembered mouse

On our back doorstep this morning.

Its tiny, orange stomach protruding

Like a small, inflated water balloon.

I think it's a threat because

We ran out of kibble.

If you don't hear from me…

…send help!

LIFE

I've gone back

To square one

So many times

That I've put

A sofa, T.V

And bookshelf there.

JANUARY PRAYER

Dear God,

I'm feeling proper rough today! Despite friends praying for me, I seem to have got worse. I don't understand.

However, I just want to thank you so much for your provision and for all your goodness.

Thank you for Christ's death for me. That Jesus would be slapped, mocked and humiliated *for me.* Thank you.

The bills are increasing and the greedy are prospering, while the needy struggle. Please help me trust you. You are God and are in control. Your word says you provide for even the sparrows. Thank you.

You are all powerful, all knowing and present everywhere. You are goodness, mercy and kindness. Praise your name.

Please bring healing to my body.

I pray all these things in Jesus' name and according to your perfect will.

Calum

ARABESQUE

Arm reaching out.

Leg extended behind;

A position about yearning.

A constant pull of the limbs

Away from one another,

Reaching for what's just

Beyond our…

Grasp.

RISK-TAKING

Today

I went on a train.

Despite

Knowing all that could go

Wrong

I left my safe village and

Ventured out,

Even though the tremors in my hand

Whispered

That I was still

Scared.

WARY

The imprint of his bum

Is still in his armchair,

Which the cats don't seem

To want to sit on.

CURVE-BALL

It left me perfectly perplexed

And decidedly discombobulated

After I'd shared a poem about being proud of what I had achieved....

'Who do you think you are?'

Well that's a big question.

Thanks Mum!

PLEASE REMEMBER ME...

Breathe me

Back to life

Tell stories

Of silliness and woe

That way

I'll live forever

And you don't have

To let me go.

SIMPLE PLEASURES

Bread and jam.

Jam and bread.

'Nuff said.

WAVES

Stephen Hawking explained that

when Two waves meet,

They either enhance or diminish

Each other.

I think people

Are like that too.

BABY BLUES

The blue buttons

Shone

Polished by his mammy;

Perfectly piercing

Just like his bonnie blues.

His skin,

(Still a shade of grey)

Wasn't quite perfect

But his blue buttons shone,

Despite the forlorn clouds

When we said goodbye

To my baby on that day.

CALL OF THE WILD

Where are the wild women

With twigs and nests in their hair

and feral claws;

Hearts that love ferociously?

Where are the wild women

With wide hips and roars of ecstasy

And anger;

Bodies that grip tightly?

Where are the wild women

With rooted, strong legs

and berry-juiced lips;

Minds that think creatively?

Where are the wild women

With calloused, scarred hands

And soil covered feet;

Eyes that perceive and pierce?

Where are the women who do not hold back, who scratch, who soothe, who bite, who achieve and surpass and write and protect?

Where are the wild women?

IRONING

I glide it across the surface

Creating a hovercraft, floating on steam

As waves and ripples disappear

While I gently turn and pull with my left,

As the ships prow is pushed across a white ocean, spraying water ahead of it;

Forging a path, that soaks,

Dries, then smooths.

Turning the shabby and disheveled into

Perfectly, pristine, perfection.

Collar to cuff.

Tail to button hole.

As the ship glides and forges ripples and waves into disappearing

With a hiss, a spit and a sigh.

SOME PEOPLE KNOW WHAT IT'S LIKE TO BE ON BENEFITS....

To dread receiving presents because you can't afford to buy them in return.

To awkwardly change the subject when someone asks you what you do.

To be invited for a meal knowing the money could feed your whole family for a week.

To say thank you every month for gifted food and clothes you desperately need.

To have your kids mocked at school because you don't have a car.

To buy most clothes second hand and buy clothes for yourself every other year.

To find twenty different free things to do in the holidays, while scrolling social media, looking at friends enjoying days out and holidays.

To have you and your kids regularly reminded that they're 'pupil premium'.

To debate whether you need loo roll or washing up liquid more.

To use three blankets on the kids' beds, duvets in the lounge and gaffa tape on the windows to avoid putting on the heating....

To constantly put pride, embarrassment and shame aside in asking for or accepting things because it's for the kids and they come first....

.....And some people don't.

SAVING GRACE

The alert light flashed

As nurses rushed to room ten

Grace had sliced open

Her veins again.

We had checked

The room

For sharp objects

And rope;

Although sadly

It didn't change

Her lack of hope.

The doctor rushed in

Face, white as could be

...she'd died, aged thirteen

And used a broken C.D.

THERAPY

Someone

Else to

Let me down

ELEPHANT IN THE ROOM

(And on my chest)

There's an elephant in the room

And it's sat on my chest.

Feeling out of breath

My heart's bursting through my vest.

I can't rest,

Pulse races,

Nervous about faces.

A trip to the store is as daunting

As a day at the races;

Crowds or shops

Can't stop - the shakes start in my hand.

Nellie sits on my chest

I don't feel like I can stand.

Not planned

Not scheduled

I want my money back

There's an elephant on my chest

Called panic attack.

HEAVY ON THE MAKE-UP

Applying Touché Eclat

To hide the bruise

Around her left eye

And down her nose.

Wincing as she applies

More concealer

Her face hurts,

Not from the eye-watering

Pain to touch her skin

But from the weight of the mask

That's wearing thin.

SINKING TO THEIR LEVEL (IN SHAKESPEAREAN)

I pray thee pay attention

For when though dost

Duel or disagree with a vain,

Motley-minded ape

That verily, others doth

Not confuse thee with

Each other.

THIN SKINNED

The pain feels overwhelming

And her heart is permanently sore.

As though all the armour's been worn away

And every feeling is too raw.

SELF-DOUBT

I used to spend

most of my days

worrying

If I was

Or ever would be,

enough…….

HONOUR

Between thieves

But not

Between

Politicians

FALLING ON DEAF EARS

The most painful sting

Wasn't the pain

You repeatedly caused…

It was when I said

'I forgive you' and

You didn't realise you had

Done anything wrong.

DISSONANCE

Just because

You love me

(Or think you do)

Doesn't mean

I feel loved by

You.

BEN-NEVIS

1. What do you call yourself?
2. Which season do you prefer?
3. Are there secrets inside you?
4. Do you feel pride at being the tallest in Britain?
5. How and when were you formed?
6. Do you get shorter as you age?
7. Do your tears fill Loch Nevis?
8. If you weren't a mountain, what do you wish you could be?
9. How many creatures call you home?
10. At night, are you lonely or do you converse with the other mountains through the wind?

POLITICS

Loquacious men sit

Gabbling and gobbling

Like battery farmed Christmas poultry.

Wattles wobbling

Posturing and pecking

Like the schoolyard children they still are.

TWO FACES

Sometimes, love

Isn't enough

and

Sometimes, love

Is too much.

AN UNDERSTATED, VAGUELY ROMANTIC
YORKSHIRE LOVE POEM

And so it was

As it will always

Be.

There it is.

That's that.

Just me

And thee.

THE MASTER'S WORK

Cerulean sky canvas;

daubed with brushstrokes of

Coral, fuschia and rose.

Dying embers glowing above;

Before the advent of

Night.

WAKE UP!

Don't say
That God isn't
Speaking to you, while
Your Bible is closed.

OPEN AND SHUT CASE

A lot of people I know

Are '*open*-minded',

Accepting, tolerant

Folk…

…Who are *close*-minded,

To even the slightest

Possibility, that God

Exists.

...PERSISTENCE

Some prayers are answered

Before we've even brought them to God.

Some prayers are answered

Quickly; within hours, days or weeks.

Some prayers aren't answered,

Or at least are perceived to be unanswered.

Other prayers though, require patience,

Brought daily for years, while God teaches us...

SETTLED

My debt has been settled.

The price is paid.

My bill is covered.

The foundations are laid.

God sought me out.

He heard when I prayed.

My debt has been settled.

The price is paid.

DECEMBER PRAYER

Dear God,

I'm sorry I got so angry with you yesterday…my youngest's been ill lots and despite so many people praying, she keeps getting sick.

She's not been well (or sickness free) for two months now and it hurts that I can't make her well. It's also exhausting.

People keep telling me 'God's timing is perfect' but that doesn't really solve anything does it? It doesn't make my wee girl's pain go away and I'm struggling to see that you, the God who created mountains and oceans; you the God who healed people in their thousands through Jesus, couldn't just click your fingers, and make her better.

If I need to learn patience or persistence concerning myself, fine but I don't understand why my wee one has to suffer. It's been eight years God and she rarely goes a month without being ill.

Is there any point praying? Do I need a vicar to pray? Is my faith not enough? Have I got sins that are blocking my requests or should I be fasting? I'm struggling to understand.

I was told it's pointless to be angry with you but I know that! It doesn't help me though. It seems so arbitrary- one person's healed, another isn't and if we have an issue then we're told 'No-one knows God's plan and here's a bunch of guilt-inducing questions'.

I know beyond know beyond know, you provide and have looked after us in these four months since becoming Christians but why, why is this one main issue not changing?

I'm sorry but it's always going to be a sensitive issue with my kids. I'll trust you and I know you're with us but please help make her well or get the docs to work out what's wrong.

Thank you for always listening to me.

Calum x

A CHILD MAKES A WAY

We celebrate Christmas as

God came to earth;

God sent his son

In a humble birth

In a stable-come-cowshed

In the dirt and hay.

God became flesh

Who would one day say

'I am the way.'

The virgin mother and

Angels declaring to shepherds

Reverent and bowed

With trumpets blaring.

Then wise men from the east,

Bearing gifts that were odd

But symbolised the future

Of the son of God.

Where a mother held her son,

Tears of joy as she'd pray,

Thanking God for the one that would say

'I am the way.'

A SCOTTISH POEM ABOUT BEING TIRED

Today I struggled

With feeling puggled!

POPPY

A bullet hole

Pooled with blood.

A dark haired woman, viewed from above, dancing with twirling, scarlet fabrics,

The pupil of an eye,

Reddened by grief.

A solitary man, viewed from above,

In a field of crimson flowers.

A commemoration.

A symbol.

A reminder life can grow, where lives were ended all too soon.

STICKS AND STONES

Daniel sat in the corner and cried,

He didn't whimper,

He didn't get angry;

As though,

That one comment broke his last resolve.

He gave up,

Curled up

And cried.

The day that part of Daniel

Died.

HAPPY PLACE

Nuzzle my face in your hair
My love.
Nuzzle my face in your hair.
I don't give a damn
While I dance with my lamb
And I nuzzle my face in your hair.
Nuzzle my face
While the world goes by.
Nuzzle my face in your hair.
You're holding me tight
But with you I'm alright.
Nuzzle my face in your hair.
Nuzzle my face in your hair
My heart,
Nuzzle my face in your hair.
The day can be night
But with you I'm alright
While I nuzzle my face in your hair.

VALUE

Labels are useful

If you're a product,

Waiting to be bought

So others can know

Your price;

For most of us though,

They only cause us

To question our

Worth.

SURROUNDED

There's wonderful, incredible, omnipresent

And divine

Stories all around us

All of the time;

In the lines of a rust-red leaf

To a spider's artistic web.

In the veins on bark

To the waves that ebb.

In the buzzing of a bee

Or the layers of a rose

We're surrounded constantly

By poetry and prose.

MORNING WALK, WITH MY ELDEST DAUGHTER, TO THE LIBRARY

We walk in silence

Before starting to notice the beauty

Of this sunny, chilly, Autumn morning.

Three shades of green in one hedge.

Yellow, brown and orange leaves

Carpeting the floor,

Like a beautiful, middle-eastern rug.

Leaves falling and fluttering from trees

Like hundreds of butterflies

Surrounding my daughter and I.

Clouds morphing and metamorphosing

Into people, creatures and shapes.

The sun blinds us as we look away,

Only to notice a blue-grey moon, winking.

'And the heavens declare the glory of God'

TEN QUESTIONS I ASKED THE SEA:

1. Are you one creature or several
2. How do you feel as your tides ebb and flow?
3. What is your favourite time of day?
4. Do boats itch or tickle?
5. How does freezing to ice feel?
6. What do you call yourself?
7.Are you ever lonely?
8. What are your favourite sounds; children playing, the spray of whales, dolphin squeaks... or something else?
9. Does sand make you itchy?
10. Were you and the moon once lovers?

STRENGTH

After an eternity,

She whispered

'Stop!'

RUACH

Hushing and whispering.

A stirred soul.

Shalom (peace)

A yearning for God's presence.

Present.

Now.

God the Holy Spirit.

Ruach.

ONE SONG TO PLAY AT MY FUNERAL

'Don't.

You.

Forget.

About.

Me.'

.......cue congregation standing with their fists in the air.

DAMAGED PERSPECTIVE -

I was raped
When I was five;
It made my
Perspective distorted
So whatever the world
Had planned for me,
It was always
Going to be
Thwarted.

(This is about the sexual abuse I experienced at the hands of older children - written in 2021, at least a year before becoming a Christian)

SELF MOTIVATION

Tin man,

Hollow sound,

I'm banging on my chest,

Stamp the floor,

Hear me roar,

My words are manifest

And I don't compare my self

Though you do,

This isn't a hoodoo,

You could do what I do

But when I raise my intentions,

Busting out my vest

I must attest,

When pressed,

I bang on my chest.

Silverback, Haka chant,

I declare it, because I still,

Send my words out with power;

God can. God will.

POETRY-HOP

This is hip hop

Pop til you drop

Perfect prose

That's never gonna stop

Jumping, thumping

Words jostling and bumping

Sentence roads

That I have to put the humps in

Bouncy, uneven

Adjective affliction

Can't help but feed

My lexicon addiction

Powerful words

Creating senses,

Leaping over towns, buildings, fences

This is hip hop

The rhymes won't stop

Words drop, rhymes pop

Now back to the top.

BE

Be kind. Be caring. Be considerate. Be grateful. Be interested. Be present. Be loving. Be understanding. Be there. Be real. **Be kind.** Be generous. Be aware. Be smiling. Be daring. Be defiant. Be brave. Be yourself. **Be kind.** Be open. Be magical. Be gutsy. Be honest. Be faithful. Be genuine. Be still. Be quiet. Be original. Be you. **Be kind.** Be-lieve.

Be.

Be.

Be.

Be kind.

Be here now.

Be.

KINTSUGI

With every fracture, break, crack and chipped off pieces,

You are being pieced back together

With gold, by God;

When it's painful and difficult or a situation or person feels too much to face,

know that God cares, God listens and

You will be stronger, more beautiful

And more special

Than before.

('**Kintsugi** is the Japanese art of putting broken pottery pieces back together with gold — built on the idea that in embracing flaws and imperfections, you can create an even stronger, more beautiful piece of art.')

SOME POEMS...

Some poems are meant to be shouted;
A rallying cry from the rooftops.

Some poems are meant to be whispered;
Raw rhythms for those who will listen.

Some poems are meant to only be read;
Eyes drinking in each phrase and word.

Some poems are meant only to be prayed;
Praising and petitioning a God who loves you.

Some poems are only meant for your family;
Memories or word-pictures shared.

Some poems are the unsaid ebb and flow;
Silence and glances between kindred spirits.

Some poems aren't meant to be written;
Their truths too honest; too real.

Some poems are word doodles and play;
Sketching phrases or making words dance.

Some poems are thought-organisers;
In writing them we understand more.

Some poems are articulation of God's work;
Helping others see a glimpse of his greatness.

Some poems are meant to be cherished;
To be loved or clung onto, in times of need.

Some poems change and metamorphose;
We need to re-read them as we age, change…

…and grow.

POOR PROPAGANDA

A note...

...To those who think the Bible is propaganda; made up, idealised, ideas that promote a perfect religion...

...Jesus' bloodline included a prostitute, a murderer, non-Jews and a woman who tricked her father-in-law into sleeping with her.

God's chosen people rebelled against him and complained a lot; made images of gold to worship and, despite all God did for them, forgot and rebelled over and over again.

Jesus' twelve followers were quick to panic, constantly misunderstood him; were competitive and short tempered AND when Jesus was arrested every, single, one of them ran away, after making repeated promises that they'd do anything for him...

...one of his three closest friends even denied knowing him three times.

Jesus constantly clashed with the religious elite; spending lots of time with prostitutes, lepers and tax collectors.

Jesus went against cultural and religious norms; even talking to an unmarried woman in public.

A woman was the first person to see Jesus after he came back to life, in a culture where a woman's testimony was inadmissible in court.

In fact, two books of the bible are named after women AND in the New Testament several women are mentioned as church leaders...unheard of at the time...

Pick up the Bible and read all this for yourself because, *of its time, culturally*, it's an awful piece of propaganda!

If, as some people have suggested to me, this book was made up by men who put it together then frankly, on multiple levels, they did an awful job!

See I look at the Bible and I see failure upon failure by (seriously) flawed individuals.

I see broken words; people giving in to temptation; I see a Jesus who broke cultural norms and a host of arguments and disagreements in the early church (the books in the second half of the New Testament)

I see envy, legalism, church leaders arguing and rival factions among believers.

There's simply no way this would be used as a document to show people the message of God if it was a lie.

As a piece of propaganda, this is poor.

ADVERTS

You are not enough,

You are incomplete,

You aren't attractive enough,

You don't have enough...

Unless you buy THIS!

JAMES BROWN TELLS HIS KIDS THE ONLY EXCITING NEWS FROM HIS DAY

Papa's

Got

A

Brand

New

Bag.

HEAVYWEIGHT CHINA DOLL

(A toddler learns to walk in a car park)

Blocking the way out the car park

There she stood:

China-doll eyes

With Popeyes arms

In a peach dress.

Both angry and determined

Like a heavyweight boxer getting up

On the 8th count

Swaying in an imperceptible breeze

Trying to lift her left leg,

Moving one step further-

Learning to walk.

I wanted to tell her

That with two clenched fists

And a determination to keep going,

She can have all she wants

in life

But that I also hope that when

She's exhausted, spent, in need of a rest,

That someone will again come to her,

Like her dad, and say

'I'll carry you.'

CONVINCING MY WIFE THAT I THINK SHE'S GORGEOUS........IN SHAKESPEAREAN

Oh disbelieving wench

Thy mind doth deceiveth thee.

Thou mistress of mine heart,

Thou muse of words and song;

I pray thee

Believeth me

When I dost sayeth,

Thou art the comeliest

Most ornate, quaint, wench

In this fair land!

Forever thine,

Thy husband Xxx

A LESSON I WISH I'D LEARNED YEARS AGO...

Why is there so little writing about silence

In the Christian faith?

It's literally there in The Bible;

'Be still and know that I am God.'

There's thousands of (important) books on

Prayer, worship, healing and Bible study...

But where are the books explaining how to

Sit still, focus and listen...

How to just 'be' and sit in your home or garden or in a park, thanking God.

I spent so many years in my teens and twenties obsessed with doing and doing...

When what God really wanted was for me to

Sit with him and know he is God.

COME GATHER WILD THINGS WITH ME

Come with me to the sea shore;

We'll pick wild things there.

Stones, shells, salt, purpose…

Silence;

Just being aware.

Aware of God

And how small we are.

Aware of how calm the world can be-

In the moment,

Not rushing,

Just the hushing of waves.

Come,

Gather wild things,

With me.

TESTIMONY

I'm going to share my story of how and why I became a
Christian; a decision that surprised me, as well as my family.

I was born into a family, where there was a lot of instability.
My dad was a con-man, thief, violent football hooligan and
serial cheat. My mum was a teenage mum. They both drank a
lot, partied hard and had arguments, where things were
smashed or broken.

Things came to a head in 1984 when my dad was arrested for
a fraud related offense, being put in cells in a jail in
Yorkshire to await sentencing on the Monday. On the Sunday
morning, an ex-cat burglar came in to speak to the other men
about God. The men mocked him, with my dad being the
loudest heckler.

He left the men with copies of The Gospel of John from the
Bible and left. Bored, my dad read it overnight; by the next
morning he realised he'd like to know this Jesus character
and went to track down the man who'd come in.

To cut a long story short, he found Leeds City Mission, asked
God to forgive his sins and recognised he needed God in the
driving seat of his life. The change was immediate - even
through my six year old eyes I noticed that Dad suddenly

stopped swearing, smoking, drinking and smashing the house up.

My mum, thoroughly confused, asked someone from Leeds City Mission to come and explain what had happened; so a week after my dad became a Christian, while dad was out, she met with a guy from LCM and decided to follow God.

My family life became much calmer, with my parents feeling called to train at Bible College, with a view to training to lead churches.

The next ten years were mostly calm. I heard the Christian message many times and saw lots of answers to prayer. However as I went to High School, I'd decided I wasn't interested, even if I thought it was probably true. It was embarrassing and, even though I went to Christian youth camps each summer from the age of fourteen, God could keep his religion to himself.

I had decided during high school that rather than Christianity or 'following Jesus', I only wanted to do two things in life: be a professional actor and travel the world. I'd had some professional acting work as a teenager but had only been to France.

At the age of sixteen my parents took me to see a Christian musical, toured with young people performing at an incredibly high standard. They put out a call for volunteers at the end of the show, also mentioning the European destinations they toured.

My mum and dad cannily encouraged me to sign up for a tour of the U.K, Netherlands and Denmark, which they generously paid for. Two weeks into the tour I asked God to forgive my sins and committed to living for him.

When I came home, I was calmer, less angry and treated my sisters differently, having not been the kindest sibling. I struggled with suicidal thoughts, having done so from the age of thirteen but just presumed most people did. I never talked about it with anyone.

Shortly before my seventeenth birthday, I learned of an opportunity to do a year's voluntary work in Manchester with 'The Pais Project', an organisation that went in to schools telling them about Jesus. (They're now in six continents of the world) My Hope was to use my performing arts background to serve God.

Following this year I completed a year of evangelism training with London City Mission; studying the Bible, helping run community projects and how to teach God's word.

During the year in London, I felt I needed to sharpen my drama skills to give God my best so I applied to drama schools across the country. The only one that accepted me was Riverside Performing Arts in Birmingham; a place I'd said I never wanted to live

During my year there my parents' divorce came through and my mental health became much worse. In January 1998 I tried killing my self, being told that if I'd been found an hour later, I'd have died.

After drama school I started a degree in youth work, including another suicide attempt in 1999, at the end of my first year. Things seemed relatively calm until third year, apart from the thoughts in my head daring me to end my life daily.

During my third year of university I moved back into halls, on campus and started feeling exhausted in my faith. I'd constantly beat myself up for not praying or reading the Bible enough. It was under this weight of guilt I started thinking that all the non Christians seemed freer. I started dating a non-Christian girl and turned my back on my faith.

In the twenty-two years I was away from God I tried lots of things that I thought would make me happy. It didn't matter how much alcohol, drugs or sleeping around I tried, I kept feeling empty. I got married, then divorced. I traveled the world, only to find it didn't give me any sense of peace or meaning.

I tried ending my life again and also started self-harming. The daily taunts to kill myself didn't let up, regardless of medication or counselling. I tried training as a cage fighter for a year but that just stoked my constant anger and rage that bubbled.

I tried having a career, teaching Drama and English for thirteen years, which merely left me feeling numb. I quit the profession in 2019 due to the damage it was doing to my mental health; I'd come too close to jumping on the rail tracks during my morning commute.

I'd convinced myself God probably didn't exist. I hated even the mention of his name; I'd block or unfriend old friends for posting about him.

I got married a second time, having met my wife, Laura, through a work colleague. Regardless of how happy we were, my mental health was still a struggle and in December 2021 we were ready to divorce.

By some miracle, we stayed together and gave it one last try. For the past couple of years I'd been reading a lot to distract myself from the endless stream of paranoid, suicidal and dark thoughts. I read classics, books on different faiths and philosophy.

I also explored the occult and new age; ouija boards, tarot, Wicca and Yoga; nothing made a difference to the emptiness I felt. again, nothing I found gave me any sense of meaning or peace.

I constantly felt angry, irritable and on edge. Don't get me wrong, I loved and do love being a husband and dad but there was still no peace. One day I decided to try exploring Christianity and whether God existed again; my logic being that I'd read up on most other things, including Richard Dawkins' 'The God Delusion', which I'd hated.

Walking home from the local supermarket one day I mumbled a prayer to God:

'God if you're there please help me understand. I don't think you are but if by some chance you are, prove it.'

As I reached the door of my house a verse popped into my head that I'd last thought of decades ago, 'Be still and know that I am God' from Psalm 46:10. A little freaked out I told my wife, then committed to reading about 'this God', who I'd long forgotten.

I found a book by Lee Strobel, a former journalist and law graduate. He had set out to disprove the bible and God, when his wife became a Christian. Applying his journalistic eye, he spoke to experts in various fields only to realise the evidence proved God was real. His books 'The Case for Christ' (which has since been made into a movie) and 'Case for Faith' seriously challenged my strongly held beliefs.

I next decided to look into people's stories, intentionally reading books that covered different ages, backgrounds, genders and ethnicities. The same words kept cropping up time and time again; 'peace', 'acceptance', 'meaning', 'freedom' and 'healing'.

After a week or two I gave in. The evidence seemed overwhelming and despite still having a few questions I sat on my back door step one afternoon and asked God to forgive my sins. I told him I wanted him to be in the driving seat of my life and that I'd serve him in whichever way he saw fit.

My wife and kids, surprised at my decision, saw an immediate change. I stopped swearing, having previously used swearing as verbal punctuation. I felt the anger and irritability evaporate during those first twenty-four hours.

Laura, my wife, became a Christian a week later due, in part, to the change she'd seen in me. We started praying together each evening and started communicating more than we had ever done. The kids noticed a big difference commenting that we just seemed 'happier'.

Since becoming a Christian I have a peace and contentment I never had before. The biggest changes have been regarding the hopelessness and dread I constantly felt before, which have gone. I love reading the Bible and find new and amazing things in it daily.

A lot of the changes that God's made aren't obviously clear, as my wife and I had long since put partying/getting drunk/clubbing behind us. Some of the biggest changes have been how we handle conflict and I think we love each other more.

It's changed how I am as a dad. I'm more patient and less reactive. I'm more inclined to forgive the kids and not hold grudges, which I'd struggled with before.

My attitude to sin is different- I hate it. I hate messing up because I know God's holy and I want to live for him.

Do I still mess up? Absolutely. My anger and swearing have mostly gone but it occasionally surfaces and explodes; one of the hardest lessons has been to keep confessing to God, then trusting that forgiveness instead of distancing myself, in shame, as I'd done when younger.

I have a hope and solid foundation in life now, where before it felt so bleak and meaningless. I was so scared that eventually I'd lose the battle with my mental health. I know

I'm going to heaven one day and I know that, while on earth, I have a relationship with God, who is with me.

Since the age of 13, I don't think I have had a week where I haven't had a suicidal thought; Since giving my life to God, I've only had one. That's a miracle I could never have imagined before. Praise God!

If there's a verse that summarises my approach to life now, as opposed to before recommitting my life to God, it's this:

'I shall not die but live, and declare the works of the Lord.' Psalm 118 v 17

I don't want to die anymore and this book, in part, is my attempt to declare the amazing, wonderful, loving, life-changing works of God. My story and this book really are a series of notes about God's grace.

Calum 2023

A FINAL WORD

Well we made it! How was it? Thank you for reading and buying this book. It really does mean a lot. If you've enjoyed it please review it on Amazon and Goodreads (and anywhere else) ; it makes a huge difference for self-published authors as we don't have publicity and advertising budgets.

If you'd like to follow me or find me online for more poetry and thoughts, my accounts are:

TikTok: @gospelinthegarden

Instagram: @gospelfrommygarden

@gospelfrommygarden_

I always appreciate photos of people with their books,or just the books when they arrive, to share online.

If you're a Christian and think this book would help another believer or just make them smile, please recommend this book (or even buy another copy to give away).

Lastly, if you don't know God or have a relationship with him, please at least investigate it. It's of utmost importance. The reading list I've included is by authors who are far better at explaining faith, evidence and the Christian message than me.

The Bible and God can stand up to scrutiny; and maybe, like me, you might be more than surprised at what you find.

Calum Mackenzie 2023

ACKNOWLEDGEMENTS

Firstly, a huge thank you to my wife, Laura who's my champion, cheerleader, editor and uploader. You're the person I'm most grateful to God for.

Secondly I'd like to thank every single person who bought, shared and reviewed my first poetry collection, which raised money for the mental health charity 'Mind'.

It was a real boost and encouragement. I will always be grateful. Thank you for buying THIS book you're holding too. That people own writing I've done is still mind blowing.

Thirdly, I'd like to thank the people who've encouraged my family and I in these first 14 months of being a Christian; my old London City Mission V.E friends, the Northampton lot, Birmingham friends, PAIS people and anyone else who's joined me in prayer when we've asked.

Last, but not least, I'd like to thank God who has forgiven, loved and saved me. This is all for him and any writing ability or creativity I have is due to his abundant generosity.

FURTHER READING

'The Case for Christ: A journalist's personal investigation of the evidence for Jesus.' Lee Strobel. Zondervan.

'The Case for Faith: A journalist explores the toughest objections to Christianity.' Lee Strobel. Zondervan.

'Cold-Case Christianity: A Homicide Detective Investigates the Claims of the Gospels' J.Warner Wallace. David C Cook Publishing Company.

'No Compromise: the life story of Keith Green.' Melody Green. Harvest House Publishers.

'God's smuggler: one man's mission to change the world.' Brother Andrew. Hodder & Stoughton.

'A passion for life: real life stories about faith.' D.J Carswell. 10Publishing.

'Life change: 16 men tell their extraordinary stories.' Mark Elsdon-Dew. Hodder & Stoughton.

'Why Jesus?' Nicky Gumbel. Harperchristian Resources.
'The hiding place.' Corrie Ten Boom. Hodder & Stoughton.

'Chasing the dragon.' Jackie Pullinger. Hodder & Stoughton.

'Run baby run.' Nicky Cruz. Hodder & Stoughton.

'The purpose driven life: what on earth am I here for?' Rick Warren. Zondervan.

'What's so amazing about Grace?' Philip Yancey. Zondervan.

'The Jesus I never knew.' Philip Yancey. Zondervan.

'The Shack.' W Paul Young. Hodder & Stoughton.

'More than a carpenter.' Josh & Sean McDowell. Authentic.

'Who moved the stone?' Frank Morison. Authentic.

'The Bible': The *'***New International Version***'* or *'***The Message***'* are versions that use straightforward language, rather than 'thee' and 'thou'.

HELPFUL WEBSITES AND PHONE NUMBERS

The Leprosy Mission

www.leprosymission.org.uk

Open Doors U.K

www.opendoorsuk.org

Samaritans

www.Samaritans.org

Tel (24 hour line): 116 123

SMS: Text 'SHOUT' to 85258

If you are struggling with dark, destructive or suicidal thoughts, please contact your doctor a.s.a.p and ask for help.

Mental Health Foundation

www.mentalhealth.org.uk

Mind (Mental health charity)

www.mind.org.uk

Alpha Courses

www.alpha.org.uk

For further Christian books/resources:

www.eden.co.uk

Re-vived.com

Printed in Great Britain
by Amazon

31731299R00198